Advance praise for

Wearing Smaller Shoes

Chip Haynes new book, *Wearing Smaller
Shoes* is packed full of information on living lite
in suburbia through a simple formula: reduce, reuse,
recycle and refuse. Chip shows it is possible to make
important changes in your lifestyle without a major
reorganization of your life. Pick up *Wearing
Smaller Shoes* and begin a tranformation
right from where you're sitting.

— Eric Miller, Publisher,
The New Colonist

Chip Haynes is a talented and persuasive
writer who convinces me that broccoli
tastes better than ice cream.

— Jeff Klinkenberg,
St. Petersburg Times

Wearing Smaller Shoes

LIVING LIGHT ON THE BIG BLUE MARBLE

Chip Haynes

NEW SOCIETY PUBLISHERS

Cataloging in Publication Data:
A catalog record for this publication is available
from the National Library of Canada.

Cover design by Diane McIntosh.
Image: ECOboot art by Chip Haynes.
All interior photos by Chip Haynes,
Joann Haynes and Bill Kocsis.

Printed in Canada by Friesens.
First printing August 2009.

ISBN: 978-0-86571-657-5

Inquiries regarding requests to reprint
all or part of *Wearing Smaller Shoes* should be addressed to
New Society Publishers at the address below.

To order directly from the publishers,
please call toll-free (North America) 1-800-567-6772,
or order online at www.newsociety.com

Any other inquiries can be directed by mail to:
New Society Publishers
P.O. Box 189, Gabriola Island, BC V0R 1X0, Canada
(250) 247-9737

New Society Publishers' mission is to publish books that contribute
in fundamental ways to building an ecologically sustainable and just
society, and to do so with the least possible impact on the environment,
in a manner that models this vision. We are committed to doing this
not just through education, but through action. This book is one step
toward ending global deforestation and climate change. It is printed on
Forest Stewardship Council-certified acid-free paper that is 100% post-
consumer recycled (100% old growth forest-free), processed chlorine
free, and printed with vegetable-based, low-VOC inks, with covers
produced using FSC-certified stock. Additionally, New Society purchases
carbon offsets based on an annual audit, operating with a carbon-
neutral footprint. For further information, or to browse our full list of
books and purchase securely, visit our website at: www.newsociety.com

NEW SOCIETY PUBLISHERS
www.newsociety.com

Mixed Sources
Cert no. SW-COC-001271
© 1996 FSC
FSC

Contents

1   Want to Leave a Smaller Footprint? 1

2   Why Would You Do This? 9

3   The Four Rs of Living Small 23

4   Saving Electricity Like Bits of String 37

5   Living Small *and* Keeping Your Cool 77

6   Saving Water One Drop at a Time 97

7   The Joys of Solid Waste 109

8   Surviving with Smaller Transportation 125

9   The Big, er, Small Finish 167

Index 175
About the Author 183

Dedication here:

My wife, the lovely JoAnn,

this book is for you.

1

Want to Leave a Smaller Footprint?

WEAR SMALLER SHOES. Yes, it's a lame joke, but it's the lame joke that gives this book its title. With all of the interest we see these days in saving energy and resources, and all of that talk about one's "carbon footprint" and "going green," few people point out the obvious: it works out best if you get by with less. And that's what this book is all about: it's about living your life using less energy and fewer resources, without adding more of both to get by with less. Does that make sense to you? It sure does to me.

So welcome to the world of living small. It has nothing to do with height, although, yes, I am short, and everything to do with leading a life of less conspicuous (and sometimes not so conspicuous) consumption. You need to know this right up front, though: This is not about sitting there all alone in a damp cardboard box, reading someone else's discarded magazines by the flickering light of an earwax candle. (And does that paint a dismal picture or what?) This is about living your life as you live it right now, but living it using just a little bit less. That's all I ask.

1

Yes, you are going to save some serious coin if you do even a few of the things in this book. It would probably take very few changes in your life to save the price of this book every month. With a little more effort you might possibly save the price of this book every week. Dare we hope for saving the price of the book every day? A daunting task, but who am I to rule it out? For many of us (yes, even me), savings are first measured by the money saved, and I don't have a problem with that. Money saved represents both energy and resources saved, and that really is an excellent way to track your progress.

This book is not about adding more things to your already full life. It's not about having to rush right out and purchase all the latest and greatest technology, all those wild and wonderful gadgets — in other words, buying a lot to save a little. Modern technology is a wonderful thing, but all of that modern technology takes both power and resources to build, install and run. (And, yes, to throw it away when it wears out.) This is not about that at all. This is about the opposite of that. This is about leading a simpler life. Your life, but simpler. This is more about planting trees than having to cut those trees down to make room for your new solar panels. Also, I see no reason to go into debt to save money. That seems somewhat counterproductive, doesn't it? And you paid cash for this book, right? If not, we need to talk.

Chances are you can live your life as you're living it right now, but use less to get it all done. You can use less power and water around the house, and use less fuel when you travel. You can spend less, and still keep your routine. All you need is a green routine. It takes surprisingly little effort to make a few changes that will, over time, save you quite a bit of energy, resources and, yes, money. These are things that take no more time or effort to do, but pay off in the long run because you're using less as you do things just a little bit differently. And using less is better, right? Absolutely.

I'm not going to send you off to other books or web sites. You need not write for additional information. These are all easy things, simple changes, and they are all spelled out right here in this book. This is it: this is your blueprint for a simpler life and for saving yourself a bundle of time, energy and money. You can have your life and save it, too.

Ah, but what about me? How small are my shoes? I usually wear about a size 6½ or so, but you also need to know that, yes, I really do all the things I've written about in this book. This is my small life as I lead it these days, but I'm not doing this all alone. The lovely JoAnn, my wonderful wife of over twenty years, is just as zealous about living the small life (la vida tee-nie?) as I am, and she handles our extensive recycling arrangements with tremendous enthusiasm. And, yes, if you must know, she also wears smaller shoes.

I ride my bicycle to work, just as my wife both rides and walks to do much of what she does throughout her day. We also walk and ride for fun and exercise, but bicycles and foot power get us many of the places we need to go on a daily basis. That's not to say

Trees love it when you hug them.

we don't drive. We do, we just try to not drive *everywhere* and are always on the lookout for new places to *not* drive to. Walking out to dinner is a fun night out for us. (We're just a couple of crazy wild kids, aren't we?) My best friend called me a "green freak" a while back, but I don't really see it like that. These are just things we do — sensible changes we have made over time to live our lives the way we want to, and to save us time, energy, and money along the way. We still spend the money we save, but we spend it on things that are more fun. Paying the power bill is not fun. The less I have to pay there, the better.

You also need to know that we do not live all alone out in a cabin in the woods. We live in a perfectly normal house in the middle of suburbia. Our house looks like every other house around here. Well, mostly. There are those two green metal frogs bolted to the outside walls, and the two big carved Tiki idols. Oh, and the full-sized wooden bear on the front porch. Did I forget anything? Ah, yes: the big red steel mooring ball by the front door, a gift from JoAnn's brother, Cecil the sailor. Still, overall, we live in a normal, regular sort of place, surrounded by endless humanity for miles around. I'm out there mowing the yard and working in my garage like everyone else. Few people around us have any idea that our lives are any different from theirs. Few people know our deep green secret. Maybe they will after this book comes out. Oh, my.

I do honestly believe that the key to success in this is to, no pun intended, start small. There's no need to rush around and gut your house, throw out your old life, and start over with everything all at once. We sure didn't. (And we're still changing things in our lives to do better and live smaller.) Pick one or two things to change, easy things, and give them a try. If you like how that worked out, add a couple more. If you don't like how that worked out, ask yourself what you can do that you *will* like. We all do what we can, but, yes, likes and dislikes are certainly a big part of it. Some things might take a little getting used to, but changes become habit over time. Small changes over time are the key to success, I think. Big changes are a real leap of faith, and much harder to get used to.

Looking back, I think we first started by recycling newspapers. Then we changed out a few light bulbs. I bought a little folding bike at the pawnshop downtown. Small things all, but each change led to more change, and now here we are: a couple of suburban green freaks. (Or so they say.) I still say we're fairly normal, and if you met us on the street, you'd have no idea what

Cycles and recycles, all in one

sort of lives we lead. I like that. I don't have to travel incognito. Not yet, anyway. Maybe it's not so much suburban green as suburban camouflage. Hidden green. Green does come in many shades.

I will say this, though, right up front: beware of "greenwashing." Greenwashing is what happens when companies try to sell you products by making them appear environmentally sensible ("green") when they are not. While you'll see it in all manner of commercial products and advertising, greenwashing is the most glaring these days in the automotive industry and their TV commercials. Let me just say this right here: a six-thousand-pound hybrid sport utility vehicle is not, in any way, shape or form, environmentally sensible. It's not green. It just isn't, and no happy woodsy TV commercial with little furry animals and soothing acoustical guitar music is going to change that. No motor vehicle is green, not even mine, and it really is green. (A dark, metallic green.) C'est la vie. The greenest vehicle you can buy is a bicycle, but even then, it sure used a lot of energy to make and deliver. About the only way you can truly "go green" is to go walk barefoot. I'm sorry. I'm not that green. Life is a balancing act. I have my limits. I wear shoes. Even if they're small.

You'll see that greenwashing being used to sell everything from huge cars to the smallest widget spanner. It seems as though everyone and their free-range organic sock monkey has something "green" to sell you these days. Green is the new black. Green is the new buzz word in marketing just about everything, and there's little in the way of law or conscience to stop advertisers from marketing leaking tubs of burning toxic waste as "green." Caveat emptor? You bet. Sometimes literally. Beware the greenwash. You've been warned.

There is, of course, also quite the opposite. It's entirely possible to be *too* green. Don't think so? Try reading these three words: recycled toilet paper. You had to have blanched at that one. I know I did when I first saw it in the store. I stared at those words for quite some time, trying desperately to make them say something else. They never did. Now, I know what they're *meant* to say. They're meant to say toilet paper made from regular recycled paper (as opposed to, say, post-consumer toilet paper), but that's not how it comes out. No pun intended. I'll have to give it a try someday. After they change the label. Or I leave my reading glasses at home.

Take all of this greening with a grain of natural sea salt. If you question the "greenness" of any product, do your research and find out more before you lay your money on the line. There are, as it turns out, a great many shades of green. Pick the ones that suit you and be as green as you want to be. Earth tones look good on you. Really.

Now here's the part of the book where I thank a few people for being such good sports. I know most folks don't care to read this stuff, and it's certainly not what you bought the book for, so I'll make this as quick and entertaining as I possibly can.

The first thank-you must, as always, go to my wonderful wife, the very lovely JoAnn Haynes. She not only tolerates me, but embraces our small green life whole-heartedly. She makes the runs to the recycling center and walks to the grocery store. She even goes out on bicycle rides with me. Now *that's* a good sport. Thank you, my dear. I love you.

Another large thank-you goes out to Ingrid Witvoet and everyone at New Society Publishers. They have been kind and gentle and enthusiastic. Without them, you would never have heard of me. I thank them for letting me join their wondrous clan, and hope to never let them down. I am honored. Thank you, one and all.

Also, a tip of the waxed cotton cap must go to actor and activist Ed Begley, Jr. JoAnn and I were well on our way down the green path by the time *Living with Ed* came on TV, but we didn't miss an episode. Mister B. makes living green cool, and for that, I thank him. He also answers my email every time. What a guy. Thank you, sir!

Enough of this. On with the show. Let's get a little green and live a little small. You can do this. It's easy. I'll show you how, and I will promise you this right now: I will never sing "It's a Small World After All." Not ever. You're welcome.

And by the way, as I write this, today is Earth Day, April 22, 2008. Happy Earth Day to you.

This truck is green. No, really.

Why Would
You Do This?

RIGHT NOW you're living large and you're loving it. Life is good and the living is easy. But what if you could live that lovely large life and use less? (And wasn't that a tongue twister?) What if you could scale it back a bit and save a little for later? Wouldn't that be a good thing? Let's find out.

When I talk about "saving" things, I'm talking about saving money, effort and resources, for the most part. Of course, by saving these things, you are also saving your environment just a little bit as well. You're cutting down on pollution and waste and landfills and smog, not only where you are, but where all of the things we buy and use are made to begin with: at the power plants and factories around the world. A little savings here is also a little savings there, and it all adds up. Or not, if you don't. And let's not forget: everything you don't buy is something that didn't have to be shipped, often halfway around the world, just to get to you. That makes for even more resource savings and less pollution. Sometimes doing nothing is something. How Zen-like.

Once you start conserving things, all of the different kinds of savings start to pop up all over the place. It gets to be a bit of a game: How much can I save? How many ways can I save how many different things? What can I save next? For JoAnn and me, it all started out so small and innocent, we hardly noticed we'd started at all. Yes, then it all got out of hand, but that came much later. It all started with JoAnn's morning walk.

Every morning, my wonderful wife gets out and walks three miles. She's done it for years, and everyone sees her and knows her as The Girl That Walks. On her way home from that morning walk, she always buys a newspaper at a rack just a couple of blocks from our house. She does that every weekday morning. On the weekends, we usually walk out to breakfast at Tory's Café, just half a mile or so from our house. Along the way, we buy a newspaper. On Sundays, we buy two (two different ones). The thing is, buying a newspaper every day and two on Sunday starts to add up pretty quickly when you go to throw them away. And let's face it: yesterday's newspaper is today's puppy trainer. It is, quite literally, old news. So what do you do with them all the very next day?

It came to this: the newspapers were heavy, and throwing them away — that is, bagging them and drag-

Just garbage? Just recycle!

ging them out to the curb for pickup — was a chore. There had to be a better way. There was. Several local churches and all of the local recycling centers offer newspaper recycling bins. All we had to do was save up our newspapers and take them to one of these recycling bins every so often (every couple of weeks or so, as it turns out). No more heavy trash bags, no more dragging boat anchors of newsprint to the curb. Life just got a little better, and all we did was put a big tub for the old newspapers out in the garage, right by the door into the house. So it began, and the truth comes out: *she started it*. It was all JoAnn's fault. (Thank you, my dear.)

Now, initially, that's all we did, and, yes, it actually did cost us a little more to recycle the newspapers. JoAnn would put the old newspapers in the truck (they're heavy, remember?) and drive to the recycle center to dump them in a bin. She did this as she was running other errands, but still, energy (and therefore money) was used. C'est la vie. It was probably less energy (and money) than the big garbage truck was using, and we were keeping those newspapers out of the local landfill and/or incinerator. It was a start.

When most folks talk about savings, they mean saving money, and that's OK. That's a great way to keep track of what you're saving, as money saved usually does translate rather directly into energy and resources saved as well. Take our monthly power bill, for example. It was slowly creeping up and up and then up some more. I didn't think we were using more power every month — it was just costing more to use what we did. As our monthly bill began to top $100 on a regular basis, I got focused. *Seriously* focused. This had to stop. This was nuts. We started making changes in how our house was run and the things that ran in it. We changed light bulbs, unplugged stuff we didn't need, and added things that would help. Over time, that power bill came down. Way down. Despite the ever-increasing rates charged for power, I don't remember the last time we had a power bill over $35. It's been years. How's that for savings? You can do this. You can save some serious money, just through a little conservation and even less effort. It's easy. And wait until you hear how much we're saving on our garbage bill. Go team!

Look, I've already said that I don't consider myself any sort of tree-hugging green freak, but apparently I'm alone in that assessment. Maybe I am a green freak. All of my friends seem to think so, anyway. Still, we have, at last count, five functioning gasoline engines in our garage: a full-sized pickup truck, a 500cc motorcycle, a 200cc motor scooter (with sidecar!), a gas lawn mower, and a gas chain saw (because an electric chain saw does you very little good when the power is out after a storm). We sure don't sound so green now, do we? Yes, I ride my bicycle to work, and JoAnn walks to the grocery store, but we also put some miles on those gas-fired infernal combustion machines. We watch TV and I fuss in the garage and we do all of those things suburbanites do, we just do them using a little less. And if that's all it takes to be green, then, yes, we are green. I've just never thought of ourselves as all *that* green. If we ever have the guts to ditch the truck, then I'll say we're green. Don't hold your breath.

Still, every little bit helps, and when you're looking at over six billion people on planet earth, a little bit of change can make a big difference if enough people do it. We're not doing much, but we're doing our part. We're using less, living small, and helping to maybe not pollute the planet quite so much as we used to. It's no big deal. It's not a major effort on our part, it's just how we live our lives these days. But it would be amazing if everyone did it. Wow.

We live in suburbia, surrounded by even more suburbia for about fifty miles in every direction. Except for west. Nothing but the (stunningly beautiful) Gulf of Mexico out that way. Living as we do in endless suburbia, one of the big issues here, with so many people, is the question of what to do with all the garbage. It's a good question. A very valid question. An important, immediate question. The two or three million people who live around here can generate a considerable heap of trash in fairly short order, and that's on a good day. What do you do with it all? Where does it all go? We have to answer those questions over and over again, day after day, and again tomorrow.

The county where I live operates one of the largest garbage-burning power plants in the country. It's an impressive sight to see, and it makes me proud to know that we're doing that, and have been for years. This county was green before green was cool. I like that, green freak that I apparently am. Still, as you well know, just because you burn something doesn't mean it goes completely away. You still have to deal with the ash and the things that don't (or shouldn't) burn. Around here, that means landfills. And around here, landfills can be a bit problematic. There's just not that much "around here" left.

We live, you see, in the second smallest county in the state of Florida. Close to one million people live on just 280 square miles of lovely, semi-tropical sandbar between the Gulf of Mexico and Tampa Bay. That's a lot of people on not much sand. So where does all the garbage go? What doesn't go to the power plant goes to the landfill, and the landfill is about full. Then what do we do? Then we recycle like crazy. Then we all recycle like JoAnn and I are recycling right now. I figure JoAnn and I recycle about 95 percent of everything we use. That makes for very little garbage. (I figure we generate about one small bag of garbage a month. Maybe.) If everyone did that, we wouldn't have to worry about landfills so much. Wouldn't that be nice? Maybe some day. Maybe you can help. Where you live can't be much different from where we live. All communities have to worry about what they do with their garbage, and we're all running out of room. Maybe it's time to do things a little differently. A little better. A little smaller.

There's another aspect to this living-small thing. There's a dark specter lurking behind the happy, feel-good joys of conservation and recycling. It's unfortunate and unpleasant, but I'm going to have to mention it, if only briefly. I do, in advance,

A good reason to tread lightly

apologize. This will not be easy for me to write nor for you to read, but here goes. Brace yourself.

Back in the mid-1950s, a virtually unknown geologist working for Shell Oil named Marion King Hubbert found that if he plotted the production curve for an oil well, he could see that the well delivered the most oil as it reached the mid-point of its total production volume. That is, daily production peaked when it had pumped out half of all the oil it was ever going to pump. It made for a beautiful bell curve. After reaching that mid-point peak, the oil well went into a permanent decline — the downside of that bell curve. That brief high point of oil production, that mid-point peak, became known as Hubbert's Peak.

Using what he had found, Mr. Hubbert went on to plot the production curve for US oil and found that it would peak in 1970. Needless to say, Mr. Hubbert did not get invited to many parties after that, but he was right: US oil production did peak around 1970, and except for a happy little temporary bump from adding in Alaskan oil production, American oil production has been in decline ever since. It took some years, but Hubbert's unpopular peak was slowly accepted as fact.

Now, as if that weren't depressing enough, here's where it all hits the fan: Hubbert's oil production curve can be applied to a much broader plane. His production curve that originally worked for a single oil well also works for an entire oil field, any one oil-producing country, or the entire world. Each will reach a peak at the mid-point of its production and then begin to drop into a permanent decline. It just doesn't get much more depressing than that, does it?

No, wait, it does. I have focused on oil because of all that it does, but you might not be aware of all that oil does for us these days. Yes, it powers our cars and trucks, but that's not the half of it. Oil is a major part of everything we do and everything we make. Plastics come from oil. Look around you. See all of that plastic? Without oil, it wouldn't be there. None of it. Imagine a world without plastic. Kind of sparse, huh?

It gets worse. Much worse. Oil — used to produce fertilizers, herbicides, fungicides and insecticides, as well as providing power for irrigation pumps and farm machinery — has allowed per-acre crop yields to multiply by a factor of five over the last 100 years. And that, not so coincidentally, has allowed the earth's human population to multiply by a factor of five over the last 100 years. Oil has kept us fed for a century. Now what happens to all of that food production as oil starts to slowly go away? And what happens to all of those people? Now do you see why living small might be a good idea? Welcome to my world, brought to you by less oil.

Do keep in mind that we're not talking about the oil running out. It doesn't have to. It won't. Not ever. There will always be oil. All it has to do is be less available than the demand for it. The simple economic laws of supply and demand hold true for oil just as they do for anything else, with one small but critical caveat: we do not make oil. Oh, we talk about "oil production" as if it all came out of some great factory someplace, but the reality of the thing is this: We simply pump it out of the ground, ready-made. We don't make it at all. The same holds true for natural gas, coal, and uranium. All of these are non-renewable energy resources, and they all will peak. Oil may already have. Welcome to our future, here today. Welcome to a future of getting by on less, not more. Welcome to living small, whether you want to or not.

So what does this steaming pile of joy have to do with you and your smooth suburban life? Quite a bit, actually. As our energy resources peak and decline in the years ahead, we're going to see prices for everything start to rise. As a matter of fact, we already have. You can blame all of the "above-ground factors" (like war, politics, economics and mechanical breakdowns) you want, and many people do, but the simple truth comes down to that one simple rule: it's all about supply and demand, and demand is winning this race by a furlong right now. And, yes, I know that there's another economic principle that says demand will create supply, but that won't work with oil. It has taken tens of millions of years for the earth, under perfect conditions, to create the oil we have used in about 150 years. Yes, the earth is still making oil, but I doubt any of us will be able to wait that long for the next batch.

This is where you come in. The only way to win this one is to rein in our demand now, before we have to. My demand, your demand, everybody's. We began with me, and now it's your turn. You're going to have to trust me on this: it all goes much better if you do this while you still have a choice. No one likes to be forced into anything. I sure don't. JoAnn and I started to do all of this back when gas was cheap and life was good. Our lives are still good, but gas ain't cheap no more, no more. No, gas ain't cheap no more.

If living small is in your future, whether you like it or not, then maybe going green on purpose isn't such a bad idea. Getting into these small habits now, and making these small changes over time, will make your new green routine all that much easier. I can't imagine how it might have gone for us if we had made every change we made in, say, a month's time (and by force, not choice). It would have been a crash course in green, and a whole new definition of "the green flash." It would not have been as pretty. I think I like our way better: small changes over time, with time between these changes to get used to them. Ease into it all quiet like, and you'll never notice how green you really are.

Look, I'll tell you the truth about this: despite the overshadowing threat of energy depletion, the changes in our long-set ways of doing so many things that we do day in and day out, and the cost of all of those new twisty light bulbs, going green is actually fun. Yes, *fun*. It's an easy and intriguing challenge, and it will make you feel better about yourself and your life for having made a few changes and doing things just a little bit differently. I'm sorry, Kermit, but it really is easy being green. Someone had to tell you.

Amphibian or human, we are all creatures of habit. We do tend to do the same things at the same time and in the same way, day after day. This is all about having a green routine. It's all about getting into green habits that are easier on you, easier on your wallet, and easier on the planet as a whole. It's not about adding drudgery and doing stupid things you don't want to do. You don't have to do anything. You don't have to change at all. But if you did change, maybe just a little, you'd see what that change can do; you'd see the difference it would make for you and everything around you, not to mention the difference in your wallet. Now, who's up for a thicker wallet? Anyone?

For JoAnn and I, our green routine begins when we get up in the morning. We use less energy and less water right from the very start of the day. We do not start our day by turning on every light in the house, and somehow, we both ended up not needing coffee to get started or to get through the day. That's one less thing to turn on in the morning. Funny how the little things add up, but they really do.

After breakfast, I ride my bicycle three miles to work. I've been doing that for over eleven years now, and started because I thought it might be more fun than driving. I was right. It is. But my riding that bicycle to work has also allowed us to get by with just that one pickup truck as our main vehicle, without us needing a second large vehicle at all. This gets better: since we don't need that expensive second vehicle (because I ride my bike to work), JoAnn doesn't need to work to support that expensive second vehicle we don't need, so she can stay home, take care of the house, and do what she wants to do. How much money are we saving by me riding my bicycle just six miles a day? Probably

Pedaling lightly works, too!

over $8,000 a year, which is about what it costs to buy and maintain that expensive second vehicle we don't need at all. You see how the little things add up? Wow.

Even with the truck we have (and the motorcycle and motor scooter), we tend to walk and ride our bicycles more and more these days. Yes, the high price of gas is one reason we do that, but another is that it's more fun than driving. It gives us time to relax and talk and be together without having to contend with traffic. We really do get to see the world we live in and the neighborhood around us. We save money, we're having fun, and we're together. Life is good, as long as you're not stuck in traffic. Our walks in the evening are an absolute delight, and we've come to know just about every dog in the neighborhood. Oh, and, yes, most of our neighbors. I like that.

We do a lot of walking, both for exercise and just to get around (sometimes both at the same time), but we also will spend our evenings at home, crashed out in front of the TV or reading. Again, sometimes both. We are always conscious of the power we are using for everything we do, and always looking for ways to use just a little less. Not a lot, just a little. Small changes, over time, make a big difference. And no one needs to know just how green you've become.

I know a lot of people worry about their image and the way other people see them. You worry about yours, I worry about mine. Image does matter no matter what they say. If it didn't, we'd all walk around naked, and no one wants that. (Excuse me while I shudder.) So will you have to worry about what this new green-living thing will do to your personal image? Not really. Even after everything JoAnn and I have done to "green up" our home and our lives, I'd like to say that, by outward appearances, very few people could look at us and know how we live. We (I hope) don't come across as the stereotypical tree hugger. Have I ever actually hugged a tree? Only when no one was looking, and the tree didn't seem to mind. It was either that or fall down.

If you followed us around all day, you'd see that we lead fairly normal lives. What you might *not* see is that we are using a bit less energy and resources to lead those lives — and the benefits of living small come back as lower energy and resource bills, which in turn gives us more money to spend on other things. Fun things. And fun things are better, right? So what I'm going to do is lead you through my home and my life, step by step, and show you how you, too, can save some money, save some effort and, yes, save the planet. Maybe just a small portion of it. Welcome to living small.

The Four Rs
of Living Small

SOMEWHERE ALONG THE LINE, in the middle of everything else we've been doing around the house, I ended up with these four words rattling around in my head: reduce, reuse, recycle, refuse. Over and over. It was maddening. Worse than that song I promised to not sing for you. Still, when you think about it, those four words do accurately describe the whole philosophy of living small. It is all about reducing your use, reusing what you can, recycling as much as possible, and even refusing to accept (to buy or whatever) things that you honestly do not need in the first place. Reduce, reuse, recycle, refuse. Sing it with me — you know the words!

Reduce? Yes, that is, despite the irony, a very big part of it. This is where most people can make the greatest change, and the easiest. Simply use a little bit less. Not a lot, mind you, just a little. Say, ten percent. A little bit less electricity, a little bit less water, a little bit less of everything. Could you get by with a little less food? Ten percent? Maybe so. Not a lot, just a little. One tenth. JoAnn and I started with trying to generate a little less trash (those newspapers, remember?). From there, we worked on using a little less electricity for a little lower power bill. After that, it became a game we're still playing: How much less can we use and still live our lives the way we want to? How much before we say, no, that's too much. That's too big of a cut. I'll let you know when we get to that point. I'm still sniffing around the house, looking for places to save energy and money. It's a challenge, like limbo. How low can we go? Ten percent is a good start. A reasonable goal.

We have, over time, reduced our overall electrical use to one fifth of the regional average. Our water use is minimal. I went looking for a plastic bag in the house the other day and couldn't find one. (We usually do have at least a few, but fewer all the time.) We are steadily reducing the miles we put on our truck, and find our lives to be more enjoyable the less we drive (traffic here is really bad). Living small is funny that way. I keep waiting for this living-small thing to be annoying, and it never is. Well, not for us, anyway. Maybe it would be if we had to have done it all at once, or if we had been doing more to begin with, but because we chose to do it as we did and started where we did, it's an intriguing, fascinating game.

Now, do keep in mind that we do not live our lives in a bare, empty home with hollow rooms that echo. We do not sit quietly in the dark and do nothing. Quite the opposite. *Quite.* Our home is overwhelmingly full, making it easier, I suppose, to say no to even more and still have plenty to do. Yes, we still do buy and add things to our home, but we have (I hope) become somewhat more selective in our acquisitions. We're kind of out of room. That makes it easier, I guess. Still, we do look at every potential purchase in terms of how badly we really need or want it. There is a difference between the two, and just because we don't actually *need* something doesn't mean we don't really *want* it — and that doesn't mean we're going to say no. If we have a place for it, it usually comes home.

The moral here is to reduce what you can willingly, but don't get all hinky about it. Small reductions do add up, and it's better to increasingly reduce what you use over time, rather than try to reduce too much too fast and find yourself reverting back later and regretting what you threw away just last week. Baby steps. A little bit at a time. You can do this.

Peanut butter jars full of parts, and inner tubes on the handlebars

Reuse? Oh, I'm big on that despite my height. You've probably heard the old line, "Use it up, wear it out, make it do, or do without"? Well, this takes that a step further. After I've used something for its original, intended purpose and it no longer works for that, I wonder what I can use it for next? Yes, this is a form of recycling. Maybe its purest form, as it takes the least amount of energy and effort to transition an item from one use to the next. You want examples? Examples I've got aplenty.

Let's start with a quick, easy one. We get fake plastic credit cards in the mail with applications that we shred and recycle. The fake cards are of the "Your name here" variety, and maybe we could throw them in the plastics recycling bin, but they do make great bookmarks, so we save them for that. JoAnn and I always have a stack of books to read, and it's always nice to have a few extra bookmarks at the ready. These fake plastic credit cards work great for that. And they're free!

I do a lot of fussing around with bicycles (big shock there, I know), and it always grated on me to have to throw away old bicycle tubes when they could no longer be repaired. Yes, I'd remove the valve core and add it to my now endless supply thereof (and geez, Louise, how many do I really need?), but the tube itself? There must be something I could do with that. One day I was rebuilding a bicycle with drop (racing style) handlebars, and I didn't have any handlebar tape for the bike. And, since I planned to simply give the bike away, I was somewhat reluctant to go out and buy a brand-new roll of handlebar tape for a bike I was just going to offer out for free in the driveway. I did, however, have an old tube off the bike that was blown out. No way to repair that. I'd have to pitch it. It wasn't even recyclable. Then it dawned on me: I cut the valve stem section out of the tube, split the rest of it long ways, and then cut that in half long ways again. I now had two perfectly good long lengths of black rubber handlebar tape, and they worked like a charm. Strips of bicycle inner tube are stretchy, making them easy to apply, and very cushy and grippy for your hands. It was perfect! All I threw away was about two inches of the old tube where the valve stem was. Much better. Now, these days, that's all I ever use for handlebar tape. I have a nice, steady supply of the stuff from all the old tubes that can't be repaired. Reuse is good!

Broken spokes get reused as wire hangers (when I paint bike parts), the twist ties from bread wrappers hold bundles of spokes for later use and even those wide-mouth plastic peanut butter jars (low fat, of course) are perfect for storing small bike parts. Everything we recycle gets scrutinized before it goes into any recycle bin, and certainly before it's thrown away. Can we use this again for something else before it goes wherever it's going next? What else could this be? Once you start looking at everything you use in your life, reusing things from one activity in another becomes second nature and a great challenge as well. Pick it up, turn it around, and look at it again. What else could this be? Maybe I'd better save it. You never know.

And of course I reuse (or do I recycle?) entire bicycles. I'm a nut about this. Just ask my wife. We have several bicycles in our collection that came off of trash piles and at least one that was pulled out of a ditch. (For a while there, we had a nice one we pulled out of a lake!) More often than not, whatever bike I find in my travels gets fixed up and given away. I've probably given away hundreds over the years. I get them to work, then simply wheel them out to the end of the driveway with a "FREE!" sign on them. They are usually gone within minutes. I really do like

Recycle Central — such as it is.

looking up from whatever I'm working on in the garage and seeing one of my former free bikes go by with its happy new owner.
One less car, one bike at a time. Found bicycles that honestly
can't be fixed are salvaged for their usable parts to help other
bikes, and their unusable components really are recycled. I cur-
rently have an old Schwinn Typhoon frame hanging from the
rafters, in need of wheels before I give it away. Interested? I just
found a set of wheels on my morning walk. We can make this
work!

So is that reusing or recycling? I'm not sure, but I do know
my favorite T-shirts (I have two of them) are my "bicycle recycle"

shirts. The image on the front of the shirt is three bike frames linked as a triangle to three wheels, sort of like the standard recycling symbol, but with bicycles. I don't know if what I do with those old bikes is recycling or reusing, maybe both, but I do know it helps. I keep the bikes out of the trash and put them back on the road, maybe even replacing a car in the process. Go team!

When it comes to reusing stuff, batteries are the number one thing you should reuse. We're talking here about those small, round dry cell batteries you'd use in a flashlight. Old dead batteries are still full of nasty heavy metals, and dumping them in a landfill is always a bad idea. The plan here is to not only avoid putting more of anything in any landfill, but to avoid putting toxic chemicals anywhere they don't belong. Like in your drinking water (they all leach out the bottom of the landfill). Tough to argue with logic like that. Batteries do many good things, but disposing of old batteries can often go badly. Rechargable batteries are the way to go. They really do help.

So much of our modern lives runs on batteries, it's not even funny. I use batteries for all of my bicycle lights. I have a lot of bicycle lights. I use a lot of batteries. This change to using rechargeable batteries is going to take a little more effort and outlay on your part, but it's time to switch to rechargeable batteries. You can do this. It's easy, but it does take some initial homework, commitment, and expense. You're going to need to purchase a battery charger and a supply of rechargeable batteries. (Sadly, just any old regular dry cell battery is not rechargeable.) Let's take this one step at a time.

The first order of business here is to take stock of exactly how many batteries you use in your day-to-day life and what sizes all of those batteries might be. For most of us, we're talking about sizes AAA, AA, C, and D. (Was there ever a size A or B? I've never seen one.) All six of my bicycle lights use just size AAA and AA. I think we've got some flashlights around the house that take C-size batteries, and the cool vintage headlight on my Schwinn trike takes those big old classic D batteries. I knew that when I bought a recharging system, it was going to have to re-charge up to four batteries at a time of any one size. You have to know your needs, and I knew I wanted to be able to replace all of the batteries at once in any one light. Like I said: you have to take stock of your needs.

Once you've got an idea of what you'll need to recharge, it's time to go shopping. A word to the wise here: buy a seriously recognizable name-brand battery recharging system and the matching brand-name rechargeable batteries. These are batter-ies you're going to use for quite sometime, and there's a good chance the charger will only work with the brand batteries de-signed for it. Sure, you might get a real deal on an off-brand system, but what good is it if you can't get more batteries for it when the time comes? Buy a name brand you know and trust. It will work out better for you in the long run.

One thing you need to understand about batteries and elec-tric power in general: it is not, in any way, pollution free. Not usually, anyway. The power in those batteries had to come from somewhere. It had to be generated. We don't mine electricity. We don't pump it out of the ground like oil or harvest it like wheat. Unless that battery was charged by a photocell panel, wind tur-bine, or hydroelectric plant, there's a good chance that the juice in that little tin can came from a big commercial power plant using a non-renewable energy source. Whether oil, coal, natural gas, or nuclear, any way you look at it, that power was not free and was hardly green. You needed to know that. Think of it as more incentive to use less.

And, yes, even rechargeable batteries wear out over time. They stop taking a charge. When they can no longer light up your life, make sure they go to a good home. Check with your local electronics stores and battery suppliers to find out who in your area is offering a recycling or safe disposal service for dry cell batteries. Please don't simply throw them away. We've got enough problems as it is.

Recycle? Let's talk about the third "R" in that jingle. This is a biggie. This is huge. This is what everyone thinks about when they think about green living, and, yes, recycling is certainly a big part of any green routine. But still, it's only a part of it. I'm going to go into much more depth about the details of our recycling arrangements a bit later in the book. For now, let's just cover some basics, shall we?

JoAnn and I formally recycle almost a dozen different things, and informally recycle several more. By formal recycling I mean that we have a special dedicated bin for just that one item, and that's where it goes when we're done with it, to be delivered to a special recycling center at periodic intervals. (Like, when the bin is slopping over full.) Newspapers, plastic, and glass are just three examples. You'll get the whole long spine-tingling list in infinite detail in a later chapter. This is the recycling you think of when you think of recycling, isn't it? This is what we do. You should, too.

But we also do what I call informal recycling. Remember all of those things we reuse? That's informal recycling. We also have special bins around the house for combustibles (more on that later), and I keep a much larger bin in the garage for yard waste, mainly tree limbs that have fallen. We have a lot of trees. Picking up fallen limbs has become something of a form of regular exercise around our yard. Stop, bend, and pick it up. Stop, bend, and pick it up. Feel the burn! We recycle combustibles and yard waste in the fireplace both to warm that part of the house and just because it can be nice to spend the evening reading in front of a small fire. Very cozy. And after that cozy evening with a good book and a small fire, we recycle all of that brand-new cozy fireplace ash on the lawn. It's the big, cozy circle of life, Simba.

Now I know that recycling has a certain less-than-trendy image. It can come across as maybe just a little too green for some people. Not as bad as staring-at-a-roll-of-recycled-toilet-paper-on-the-grocery-store-shelf green, but still, even I have to admit there's a certain hippy-dippy earth-person-perspiration cachet about the whole thing. (Kind of spelled it out there for you, didn't I?) Get over it. Recycling is applied modern technology on the home front. Effective recycling takes a smooth, efficient, clinical system. Think about it up front, get it set up correctly, and you never have to think about it again. The key to making home recycling work is an easy-to-use system. Get it right the first time, and all of the hard work is done. And I'm here to help you get it right the first time. We'll have you recycling in no time, at least a little bit. Just you watch.

The flip side to recycling is to buy, as much as possible, recycled goods to begin with. Yes, I might draw the line at that infamous roll of recycled toilet paper, but other than that, much of what you buy is fair game. Look for information on the packaging for the recycled content of what you are buying as well as for whether or not what you're buying is recyclable. Some things can simply be used over and over. Those are the things you want to buy and use, over and over. Trust your Uncle Chippie on this one.

Once you get into this, you'll be looking at everything in terms of where it came from and where it's going to go once you're done with it. Can this be recycled? Has it been recycled already? It's like reincarnation on fast-forward. The big question to be asked before any purchase must surely be this: how am I going to get rid of this thing if I buy it? You've got to apply those four Rs and figure out, before you're stuck with it, what you're going to do with anything and everything you buy when you are done with it. It really does work out so much better in the long run. Yeah, I mostly still buy it, whatever "it" is, but at least I go into it with a plan. And sometimes, the plan even works!

Refuse? Can you just say no? Yes you can, and that's the easiest way of all. If you have less to begin with, you're living small already. The phrase "plastic pumpkins" was invented to describe the many, many (too many) things that we all buy that none of us need. We're talking about silly cheap plastic trinkets made on the far side of the world and shipped to all of the big box stores near you. These are things that you buy because they're right there, on sale, and you have a coupon. Do you need it? No, you do not. Do you want it? Not really, but hey, it's on sale! And you have a coupon! Please, for the sake of living small, just say no. How many plastic pumpkins does one person need? I mean, really. Learn to refuse. Learn to just say no. At least a little bit.

The one place where refusing can be amusing is when it comes to those ubiquitous plastic shopping bags. We first saw this as we watched Ed Begley, Jr.'s TV show *Living With Ed*, and it was a wonderful awaking for us. Ed would ride his bicycle to the local store, walk in, buy a few small items, and *refuse the shopping bag*. Wow! It was like a classic Candid Camera moment. The store clerks could never quite figure out why Ed didn't want a bag. Everyone wanted a bag. Many people wanted two. And now here's Ed, and he didn't want any bag at all? It confused them. They didn't know what to do next. Here's what they should do: hand the nice friendly (green) person the items they just bought and thank them for shopping in your store and saving you the cost of a bag. Have a nice day. Bye now!

I was so thrilled with this idea, I tried it myself. I bought my five bananas for the week (I have one for lunch every day) and told the bagger I didn't need a bag. The look I got back was so unique I had to review what I had just said. Had I not spoken English? Was it complete jibberish? (These things happen when you're me.) Did they not speak English? (These things happen, too.) More often than not, baggers put the items in plastic bags anyway, as they're convinced I could not have possibly said what I just said. No plastic bag? Blasphemy! Try it some time. It's hilarious. And thank you, Ed Begley, Jr., for the easiest way to have great fun in the checkout line by confusing the help. Oh, and if you do walk out of the store, purchased items in bare hand, don't forget the (recyclable!) receipt. I'm just saying.

These days, we never go to the store without one of those reusable canvas shopping bags or one of our many small backpacks. We keep at least one canvas shopping bag in the truck at all times and have small backpacks hanging by the door at home. We never leave home without them. Yes, it's good to have a few of those cheap plastic bags around the house when you need them, but in all honesty, you probably don't need all that many, and they are made from oil. We periodically recycle our extras. (The local grocery store takes them back. They have a big bin for them right out front.) I understand some places are already starting to charge for them. Before long, they will simply be gone (being made from oil and all). And then what will you do? Be like Ed. Be cool, have fun, and just say no to plastic shopping bags. Hilarity ensues. Every time.

Cheap plastic shopping bags aside, if you can learn to just say no to the things you don't really need, you're already well on your way to living small and being green. All things in moderation, and some things not at all. Not a bad way to get started. If you have the nerve to turn down that sale of the century, even when they send you a coupon, you're going to do very well at this. Even on sale, you'll still have to buy it and you still have to deal with it. And eventually, you're going to have to dispose of it. Even if you got it for free, you'll have to get rid of it someday, right? If you can refuse what you don't need, the rest will be easy.

Reduce, reuse, recycle, refuse. Say it with me. Let it roll off the tongue. Think of it as a sort of poetic green reality. (It does kind of rhyme, doesn't it?) You might want to stop short of spray-painting it on the side of your local big box store in big, tall, runny letters, but do take it to heart and give it a try. I'll keep coming back to these four Rs throughout the book, but now that you know them, you'll know what I'm talking about. It's the living small theme song. As opposed to...well, *you know*.

Saving Electricity Like Bits of String

L OOKING OVER MY NOTES AND OUTLINES, I have no doubt that this will be the longest chapter in this book, and that's probably appropriate. When it comes to conservation, using less electricity is often the first thing many people think of when they think of being green and living small. This can be the largest part of it all. This is also the part where the changes are the easiest to implement, your progress is the easiest to track, and the savings are the easiest to see. You get that bill once a month, and there it is: everything you spent and used, down to the last little watt. That makes it tough to ignore when the bill is big, but the savings are easy to see as it gets smaller. And it is easy to save. Just you wait and see.

This is where you're going to save money, no doubt about that. You're going to like this big chapter. This is where we save a bundle every month. As I mentioned earlier, our power bills were creeping up to over $100 a month on a regular basis, and I didn't care much for that. It seemed excessive, considering there's just the two of us. When you talk about using power, you

37

have to understand that there's the money side of it and there's the power side of it. You're using power, but it costs you money. How much money varies according to the rate the power company charges — along with all the other silly little charges they add to your bill. Still, no matter what they call it and how they charge it, you have to pay it. If you don't, the lights go out. And nobody wants that.

In this part of the world, the average suburban home uses about 1,250 kilowatts of electricity a month. Electrical power is billed by the kilowatt-hour, more often simply called a kilowatt. We use less than 250 kilowatts a month, about one fifth of the regional average. I think we're doing very well when it comes to saving (that is, not using) kilowatts. Briefly put, a kilowatt is 1,000 watt-hours. Think of it as a 100-watt light bulb left on for ten hours. That's 1,000 watts, or one kilowatt, right there. It's very easy to use up a kilowatt of power around the house, but that also means it's very easy *not* to, if you pay attention. A 40-watt light bulb, left on day and night, uses very close to one kilowatt a day. Turn it off! For all JoAnn and I have done around the house to save electricity, we still use about 8 kilowatts of power every day. Then again, we're saving

How slow can you make this go?

well over $65 a month over our previous $100-plus electric bills by making some small changes and paying more attention to what we do use.

By paying close attention to every watt, and I do mean *every* watt, you can lower your power use, and therefore your power bill. You can save energy and save money and have more fun with the money you save. And you're not even going to miss that 40-watt light bulb you left on all the time. Trust me. I don't think we even *own* a 40-watt light bulb any more. We'll talk more about those silly new twisty light bulbs here in a minute.

For the most part, what I have to say about saving power is very simple: to save power, you simply use less power. As idiotic as that sounds, it can be surprisingly difficult to do without getting sidetracked into increased technology and needs. A few people who know how JoAnn and I have arranged our lives have asked if we plan to go off the grid — that is, do we plan to generate our own power right there at home, with solar cells or wind mills? No, we do not. Yes, we did look into it, but decided to take the road less traveled, so to speak. We opted for lower power use (less need), not increased technology. The distinction is important, I think. I liken it to the electric bicycle. And I don't like the electric bicycle.

The electric bicycle uses heavy batteries and a heavy electric motor to help move the bicycle so the rider doesn't have to pedal so hard to make the bike go. The electric bicycle is heavy because it has all of those batteries and that motor, so the rider *does* need that help to keep the bike moving along. If the bike didn't have the batteries and that motor, it would be much lighter and far easier to pedal, so you wouldn't need them in the first place. Can you see where I'm headed with this one? The electric bicycle creates its own need. I would much rather own a lighter bicycle and therefore not need the increased (and heavy) technology. Doesn't that sound like a better idea? It does to me.

Even if you were to counter the argument against increased technology, increased maintenance, and the increased expense, it comes down to this: it makes no sense for us to cut back all of those wonderful big shade trees we have around our house to give room and direct sun to solar panels on the roof of the house. That would allow the house to heat up, requiring more power use to keep it cool. It would be self-defeating. I'd rather keep the trees and all of that shade. They work for free.

The whole point of living small is to live your life with less unnecessary technology, and to need (and use) less power to begin with. It's not about adding technology and using more to use less. Does that even work? It sounds odd. I do, however, need to confess that we do get by with using less because of the way our lives are arranged. I have, therefore, three confessions I need to make before we go any further. These do help explain our low power use.

Let's start with this, confession number one: we have no kids. Those of you with children know how much power, resources and money it takes to raise children. It is substantial. I am in awe of your efforts, and amazed by the results. Yes, it is possible to implement much of what I've written about in this book with a house full of kids, but you might be hard-pressed to get your total energy use down as low as we have. There are simply more of you, and everyone, no matter what their age, needs a bit of power and uses at least some precious resources. All you can do is plan accordingly, and try to get everyone to move in the same direction. Make it a group effort, and, yes, you will see results.

Confession number two: although we do live in the middle of suburbia in a warm climate, we do not have a swimming pool in the back yard. Quite a number of homes around us do have them, but we do not. To say that swimming pools take a fair amount of power and water is rather like saying the Vatican is somewhat big on religion. No argument there. Never having owned a swimming pool, I can't really tell you much that might help you save power and water when you have a big in-ground pool lurking out back. You might try draining the pool and taking up skateboarding, but that's about it. I wish I could offer you more, but I lucked out in that regard, I think: no pool. It will be interesting to see how many home swimming pools get built in the future as energy and water get ever more expensive. I expect skateboard sales to rise proportionately.

My last confession here is a bit less specific but may be far more astounding: we are not gadget freaks. That is, we are not electronic gadget freaks. You might want to sit down for this, if you are not already. We do not own a computer at home. Not shocked yet? How about this, then (brace yourself): we have never owned a cell phone. Sorry. I know that was sudden, but you need to know these things. We are not electronic gadget freaks. We do not have banks of things plugged in and/or constantly recharging. We do not own any little portable music players. We do not text-message. No video games. No big screen TV. (Oh, we have a TV, just not a monster billboard-sized one that takes up an entire wall.) No, we don't sit in the dark and hum softly to amuse ourselves, but neither have we gone overboard and bought every toy that came down the pike.

I joke that we are semi-Amish, and by today's over-gadgeted suburban standards, that's probably not far from the truth. We do have cable TV, a VCR and a DVD, but that's about the sum total of our electronic gadgetry. I still have all of my old Beatles albums. Yes, the original LPs. We have a couple of record players, including a beautiful cabinet that plays 78 rpm records. You honestly would not believe the beautiful sound that comes out of that grand machine. I think we have a CD player around here someplace, but I can't remember the last time we used it. Last Halloween? I think so. And did I mention our *rotary-dial* telephone? Very cool item, that. It works when the power goes out after a storm. That's kind of an important requirement around here. We do get some storms.

As I mentioned earlier, we keep a close watch on our monthly electric bill. Pretty simple stuff, really: down is good, up is bad. There you go. The goal, in a nutshell, is *down*. If there's any sort of sudden spike in the power bill, we want to know why. Did the rates go up? That happens (but usually not very much all at once). Sometimes the bill is for more days than usual, if the meter got read late. A bill for 32 days' worth of power is going to be substantially higher than a bill for, say, 29 days' worth. That, right there, can account for a ten percent shift in the amount due on a monthly bill, and that makes us sit up and take notice. It will say on your bill how many days you are being billed for in that cycle, and our billing also gives us the one thing you need to watch the most: kilowatts used per day. That can be the true test of how you're really doing on conserving power. We're at about 8 kilowatts a day right now. I'd be happy to see that drop to 7½. Seven a day would be amazing. Can we do it? Is there really that much fat to cut out of our already skinny system? I don't know, but I'm sure willing to play the game a bit longer to find out. What fun!

The first order of business when it comes to lowering your power bill is to figure out what you're using. This goes beyond just looking at your power bill and having your eyes bug out like a crazed cartoon character. (Although that works, too.) Start by walking into every room in your house and taking a good, long, hard look around. Look in every space. Every closet, every cupboard, every pantry, every shelf, every nook and cranny. Look everywhere. You're using power, and the odds are that you're using power in every room. Search for it, find it, and then ask yourself: do I really need to have this thing plugged in all the time? Probably not. So unplug it already. There you go. So it begins.

When I started walking around our house with an eye to unneeded electrical use, I found that we had a clock radio plugged in out in the library. (Ok, don't get all excited here: the library is just a small mother-in-law room that we've filled with books.) Still, nestled back in there next to the fiction section were the constant glowing red numbers on an old clock radio, churning away 24/7 for no good reason. Did we even need that thing on out there? We did not. It got unplugged. I think, eventually, it became a thrift store donation. Much of our old electric stuff did.

The big electric wall clock in the garage was even more obvious. Too obvious, as it turned out. At some point in the past, I had traded a broken pinball machine that someone had given me for a functioning "Official Briggs & Stratton Service Center" electric wall clock, complete with a glaringly bright back light. I figured a functional wall clock was better than a broken pinball machine. At least it took up considerably less room. I proudly plugged the clock in over my workbench and had the time of day any time I wanted it, along with a truly stunning night-light, should I decide to go sleepwalking out in the garage after the sun went down. It was my brother who saw it and pointed out that my big clock night-light was showing anyone who walked by all of the way cool toys in my garage, and he mentioned that I might not want to advertise quite so much. At least, not so late at night. Point well taken. I took the clock apart and unfastened the bulb. Problem solved, power saved. Not long after that, I realized that the big wall clock was still slurping up power night and day, even without the bright lamp on in the back. I unplugged it and started using a smaller battery-powered clock out there. The big, shiny wall clock got traded to a neighbor. Not sure what, if anything, I got in return. I did not drive a hard bargain. I'll have to ask him about that someday. Maybe he owes me something.

We went from room to room, looking at what we had and what was using power, and figuring out what it was that we really needed. What could we get by on? How little could we get by on? What would we truly miss if it were gone? When our big stove finally went to that glorious golden kitchen in the sky, we made sure our new stove did not have a clock in it. We didn't need it, so why pay for it, day after day, month after month? Yes, we did have to look around to find such a basic stove, but we did find one. We were not so lucky with the new microwave.

A classic phantom power drain. Just unplug it!

See? A real, honest-to-gosh modern microwave. We *do* use technology! JoAnn knew that she wanted a larger microwave when our little one finally gave out, and when that day came, she went to the store armed with the measurements. She wanted the biggest one she could find that would fit on the countertop, under the overhanging cabinets. Fine by me. She ran into a slight glitch in our green routine: all of the big microwaves had clocks in them. All of them. She looked everywhere. No way around it. Finally, she found the one she wanted, complete with clock, and she bought it. The solution to the unavoidable clock? We simply unplug the microwave when it's not in use, which is most of the time. Problem solved. Sometimes you can work around technology. Sometimes you can just unplug it. That works, too.

Our refrigerator, while lacking a clock, also lacks the modern (power-using) convenience of an in-door ice dispenser, water fountain, and salad bar. We can make ice in the freezer. We kept that recipe handed down from generation to generation. I can send you a copy if you like. We've got a big pitcher of water in the fridge. It takes very little to keep that topped off, ready for instant use without the constant power. But, yes, you actually have to open the door and take it out and put it back. Is that asking so much? It seems as though manufacturers are always looking for ways to use more power, not less. That you have to figure out on your own. As for the dishwasher, it uses both power and water. We have a simple fix for that: I'm the dishwasher. Problem solved right there.

So it went. We started unplugging things we didn't need. We started using things that didn't have to be plugged in all of the time, and we noticed a nice change: our power bill started to go down. We got it under $100, but then it kept going down as we changed more around the house to use less. Every item in every room: Did we need it? Did we really use it? Does it have to be plugged in? Why did we need a clock in every room? We did not. We got wise. We got lean. We got green. We got *small*.

Come to think of it, how many lights do you need in any one room? We had our fair share, and still do. All got downsized (smaller bulbs, fewer bulbs), some got unplugged, and a few were sent packing. And no, we do not stumble around in the dark. My alarm clock is battery-operated, always a good idea if the power goes out. There's no electric toothbrush in the bathroom, and I do not use an electric shaver. (Yes, I know, I have a beard, but I still shave my neck twice a week. So there.) I trim the beard itself with scissors, but occasionally (every month or so) give it an overall mowing with a rechargeable battery-powered trimmer. The trimmer stays unplugged unless in use. Every little bit saved does make a difference, and our power bill is proof of that. Look at everything, and unplug much of it. You probably don't really need it right now, do you?

Before I start to write about the next step in living small and all of the things we did around the house to use less power, I need to say something about the difference between "electric" and "electronic." While my trusty dictionary does offer substantially different definitions for these two seemingly similar words, I don't plan to bore you with either of them. I can offer you an easy way to tell them apart around your house: the electrical items in your home use no power at all when they are simply turned off. Your toaster is the perfect example. When not cremating bread to ash the moment you stop staring at it, a toaster uses not a single watt of power just sitting there. It can be plugged in, but it is inert, and not using power. And that's good. That's what you want. Too bad you don't get that with every item you've got plugged in. The electronic ones, for example.

Electronic items, it seems, have the maddening tendency to use power even when they are "off," but are still plugged into the wall outlet. This can drive you crazy if you're trying to save energy around the house, and everything looks to be "off." The TV is "off," but it's not really off. In reality, if you looked inside it, you'd see (if you could see that sort of thing) that it is still using power like mad, just to stay warmed up and ready when you turn it back "on." All you've really done, it seems, is turned off the screen itself. The rest of it is still humming away, using power. The same thing is happening with your cable TV box, the VCR, the DVD, your computer, the cell phone charger, that

One power strip can save you a lot of money — if you use it.

electric toothbrush stand, and your cat. Well, maybe not the cat so much. I think they're mostly solar-powered.

Anything that displays a glowing light when it's plugged in, even if it's not in use, is using power right now. Even without the glowing power light shining bright (in the daytime or the night), there's a good chance that anything more complex than a toaster is using power night and day just sitting there. And I'm getting to the point where I suspect the toaster as well. We'll let the cat slide for now. The solution to this insane power drain is obvious: unplug it! That's where the (big trumpet fanfare, please) power strip comes in.

Rather than spend your days (and nights) constantly plugging in and then unplugging everything around the house every time you want to use something or are finished using it, do yourself a favor: buy some power strips. Use them instead. They work well and make it all that much easier. It sure beats having to plug everything back into the wall every time you want to watch TV or use the computer or burn the toast. (And remembering to unplug it all when you're done.) We have our TV, the cable box, the VCR, and the DVD all plugged into a single power strip. When we are done watching TV for the night, the power strip gets turned off, and they all stop using power right away. It makes a world of difference in our power use and in our monthly power bill. It's really amazing. Wow.

Now, in truth, we took it one small step further. We hardly use the DVD player at all, so it isn't even plugged into the power strip most of the time. We just plug it in when we want to use it. That saves even more power, as it's not just sitting there using idle power as we watch cable TV or something on the VCR. To some small degree, that savings is offset by the nights when we want to tape a late-night show and the power strip is left on to tape that show. Sometimes, when one of us gets up late at night, we do remember to go out and turn the power strip off after the VCR is done taping. Sometimes. But not often. It's late and we're sleepy.

Using power strips is a great way to cut down on that constant, unchecked electronic power drain all around the house (*if* you remember to turn them off), but, as in the case of the DVD player, keeping these items totally unplugged to begin with is even better. And not needing them at all wins the round. Power strips really help. Power strips are your friends. You should have lots of friends.

If you want to get all heavy-handed about it, yes, you could probably get by without any TV at all, and save even more energy and money. Many people lead fine, productive, full lives with no TV at all. Or so I've been told. I have not actually *met* these people personally, nor do I know of anyone who has. Still, the rumor persists: there are people without TVs. Rather like the lost tribes of the upper Amazon who, by now, probably have cable. JoAnn and I do watch TV. I figure it's better than driving around. If watching cable TV was my worst sin, you could call me St. Chip. It's not, so don't. Just use a power strip, and we'll both be happy.

Simply getting by with less in the way of electronic toys is obviously one way of living small, but it takes a certain degree of ruthless commitment (or maniacal gamesmanship). Can you get by without the electric toothbrush? Sure, why not. How about that pasta maker? Yeah, maybe so. The timed coffee maker that has your first cup brewed fresh and hot the moment you step into the kitchen in the morning? Hey now, wait a minute there.

We have to draw the line somewhere, and everybody slaps that line down at a different spot. I must have led a totally deprived life as I've never used an electric toothbrush, always bought my pasta ready-made, and gave up caffeine years ago. (In truth, I never liked the taste of coffee. I was a tea man myself. Now you know.) Still, we all have our limits. If you really do try this, you'll find yours.

If you do decide to tough it out and start looking at living with fewer powered toys, please don't go all crazy over it. There's no need. If you eliminate just one powered gizmo a month and learn to live without that before unplugging the next one, that can be a huge savings in a year's time as you've now unplugged twelve things around the house. Way to go! (If you do.) Even six items is a leap. Even one. Maybe it's time to take a good, long look around the house and ask yourself: do I really need that? How long have I had it? It might be less painful to start with the latest toys first. The stuff you're not really used to just yet. Just a suggestion. Here's another suggestion: if you do try this, don't just unplug the item and leave it sitting right there in front of you. That's just temptation on a shelf. Unplug it and pack it away in a back closet somewhere out of sight. If, after a month or so, you've forgotten where you put it, then you really didn't need it, now, did you? Eventually, you can put all of those unplugged, unused toys in a big yard sale. Won't that be fun?

One easy way to use less power around the home here in America is to look for the blue Energy Star label on the things you buy that use power. Energy Star is a US government program that was started in the early 1990s to help American consumers use less power and lower greenhouse emissions by putting less demand on power plants around the country. (The long-range goal is to have to build fewer power plants.) The plus for us consumer types is that these things use less power, so buying them when you replace your appliances around the home will lower your power bill that much more.

So what kind of energy savings are we talking about? While there are over 40,000 products with the Energy Star label available now, here are just a few that will help you lower your home energy use: refrigerators with the Energy Star label are supposed to offer a 15% savings over the minimum standard. Dishwashers need to show a 41% savings to qualify as an Energy Star appliance. These savings will really add up as you invest in these items over time. (After all, it's not like I'm going to pop over and do your dishes for you.) I wouldn't pitch a perfectly good refrigerator just to rush right out and buy the power-saving Energy Star item, but when the time comes and your fridge goes down for the last time, this is what you look for to save even more when it is time to buy.

Energy Star TVs are supposed to use 30% less power than other TVs. That's a big savings right there, considering how much we all use our TVs, but the Energy Star models are also supposed to use less power in their standby ("off") mode. (That's for those of you who don't put your TV on a power strip.) I guess an Energy Star TV on a power strip would be the best of both worlds, wouldn't it? There you go.

Energy Star electronics (there are over 40,000 items, remember?) offer varying degrees of power savings, but overall, they seem to be one of the best deals going for saving power and money. If you have to have electronics in your home, and you probably do, go for the Energy Star items and you're going to save money as you save power. You can also buy entire Energy

Star homes, but don't let's go there just yet. For now, stay where you are and look for the blue Energy Star label when you go shopping. It's not a brand name — it's a guideline. And it helps.

One of the quickest and easiest places for anyone to save energy around the home is in their home lighting. This is where you can make some quick changes and see immediate results. More often than not, you don't have to do anything at all, and you'll save both energy and money. That is, don't turn the light on in the first place. It just doesn't get any easier than that, does it?

We have, in this modern world, become so accustomed to over-lit (artificially lit) living spaces that the idea of using just natural light is now considered a new and novel approach. The idea that you can simply throw open the curtains and have all the light you need, for free, never occurs to the average suburbanite. Me? I do it all the time. Our kitchen window, over the sink, gives me more than enough light after dinner to wash the dishes without having to turn on any light at all. Plus, I get to see what's going on outside. It's sort of like after-dinner theater, performed by an all-squirrel cast.

The rest of our house has enough windows to keep the house fairly well lit no matter what the time of day. Throw back the curtains and let the daylight in! Ah, I hear you asking, but what about at night? Doesn't it get dark at night, even in Florida? I'm glad you asked that.

Yes, we turn on lights at night. Not every light all at once, mind you, but we do, like everyone else, have a couple of lights on at night. We're not cavemen. The funny thing is, when you live in suburbia as we do, there's so much ambient light outside at night from the streetlamps and other people's outdoor home lighting that we can, if we get up late at night, wander around the house without the need to turn on a light at all. (No pets to trip over in the dark. Can you tell?) If our neighbors conserved power as we did, that would not be possible. Think they'll buy this book and turn their lights off? Oh, bother.

Rather than work to let the daylight in, you can also just go outside. It's amazing to me how many people live their lives from home to car to office and back again, never really spending much time at all outside. Their yard may as well be a foreign country. It is foreign to them, as they never go out and enjoy it, and have a yard service that takes care of it. What's the point? Get out there and roll in the grass! (When no one's looking, of course.) Make good use of all of that wonderful free daylight out there. Do something outside for a change. I think you'll like it.

In *Walden*, Thoreau wrote of taking all of his furniture out of his little cabin and arranging it outside for the day. He would spend the day out in the woods like that, and it does sound like fun. These days, we have patio furniture and deck chairs and all manner of things made to be outside. No need to drag the heavy recliner out into the back yard, although that might be fun, too. I keep a wooden folding chair by the garage door and enjoy going out in the evening and reading whatever it is that I'm reading at the time outside as the sun goes down. It's really quite relaxing. Come to think of it, I don't even own a recliner.

Not everyone has the option of going outside when it's nice (and here in Florida, it's always nice). I understand that. For many people, there are seasons to contend with, and not all seasons are outdoor seasons. Maybe you're going to be inside more than I am, and that's OK. We can work with that. We can make that work for you. All you have to do is follow one simple rule: turn the light off.

I admit I am absolutely floored when I visit other people and see how very many lights they have on all over the house all the time. It's truly astounding to me. Do they need this much light in every room? Do they see how many lights are on for no good reason? Did they forget where the switch was? Wow. Just becoming conscious of your energy use, just turning off the unnecessary lights, is a huge step toward lowering your energy use and your monthly power bill. Most folks can save ten percent right there. Maybe twenty. Just turn the light off.

JoAnn and I try to get by with one light per person. It seems a reasonable rule. We can't always do that, of course. There are times when you're doing something that really requires more light or light from more than one direction. To counter that increased use, we also share a light when we can, and that tends to offset the times when we each need more. Keep in mind, there is a line not to be crossed here. Yes, lower lights are romantic, but there's nothing romantic about whacking your leg against a table in the dark and increasing everyone's vocabulary. Nobody wants that. Fair warning there.

I wrote earlier about searching the house for unseen power use, and the lights are no exception. The one big drain few people think about would be those outdoor motion sensor lights. Those motion sensors are using power day and night, just to turn a light on for you when you're probably not looking anyway. We used to have one out over our garage door, so it would come on as we pulled up at night, and I could get out and unlock the door without having to guess which key to use. After a while, I realized I could simply leave the truck's headlights on and accomplish the same thing but use less power. Problem solved, energy saved. No more motion sensor light. How many do you have around the outside of your house? I'm just saying.

A variation on the outdoor motion sensor light problem is the indoor bathroom nightlight conundrum. We all have them, and we all use them. Still, the last thing you want to do at 3 AM is walk into the bathroom, hit a switch, and get blinded by a bazillion watts of blazing insane power. I'm not usually wearing my sunglasses at

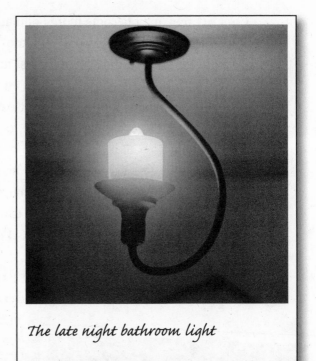

The late night bathroom light

3 AM. Not usually. Yes, I know a lot of people use a small nightlight that is simply left on all night, but that seems a bit much when you'll only need it for a couple of minutes, if that. Maybe. My solution was to fit a very small (5-watt) compact fluorescent light bulb into the overhead light fixture in the bathroom. Hit the right switch and you get a nice, soft glow to help you through the night. Hit the wrong switch, and, yes, you'll wish you had your sunglasses. I try to hit the right switch late at night. In all honesty, I use that silly little 5-watt light about 95 percent of the time I need a light in the bathroom. The only time I use the larger (48", 32-watt) fluorescent light over the big mirror is to shave my neck twice a week. Ah, the joys (and savings) of having a beard.

I suspect they may become more popular. Then what will I do to stand out? How about a forehead tattoo? Maybe not.

If I were pressed to name the most important innovation for green living in this early part of the 21st Century, I would, without hesitation, name Ed Begley, Jr. A close second would have to be the compact fluorescent light bulb, or CFL. (And I do plan to refer to them as "CFLs" from here on out, as both of my stubby little typing fingers do get tired with all of those long, complex words.) CFLs are the wonder lights that allow us to make a substantial change in our home energy use as easily as we would change a light bulb. Small joke there. It's OK, you don't have to laugh.

I say it's that easy, but, of course, there are always exceptions to the rule. When JoAnn and I began to change out the light bulbs in our house for CFLs, as we did some years ago, there honestly weren't all that many choices in CFLs. At first, you had but two: take them or leave them. Now, some years later, you can buy CFLs for virtually any home application, indoors or out. They come in a wide range of styles and wattage and can be used virtually anywhere in any lighting situation. Put them in every lamp in the house. There is no

The difference in power used is worth the money spent.

reason not to. Seriously. You can even get yellow CFL bug lights for outdoor use now. Is this a great country or what?

We did run into one small snag with my bedroom nightstand lamp. The lampshade was held in place with a double loop that slipped over a regular incandescent bulb. Those thin metal loops didn't care all that much for a standard, twisty CFL. The solution was to change how the shade was held in place, and JoAnn bought a harp with a top bolt for the shade instead. And, yes, we also had to get a new shade. C'est la vie. It looks great.

The only other problem I can recall, in all the lamps throughout our house, was with the chandelier in the hallway. Originally, it used something like eight small "candle" bulbs arranged radially from a central hub. Because of the framework that held the chandelier together, there was no room for anything wider than the bulbs it was designed for, and even now, all CFLs for that size socket (they use smaller light sockets than standard bulbs) are too wide to fit between the braces that hold the chandelier together. Until we see much narrower CFLs on the market, and I have no doubt that we will, the only solution is to simply remove six of the eight light bulbs and use the smallest wattage light bulbs we could

Our infamous chandelier. Everyone has one, it seems.

find for the other two. We still have plenty of light in the small hallway, and we still get to use the cool chandelier.

So how much are we saving? Standard CFLs offer the same amount of light (lumens) at one quarter the wattage of incandescent bulbs of the same brightness. So you save 75 percent right there. How's that for easy? They are well worth the added expense, no doubt about it. Like I said, they're the best thing since Ed Begley, Jr.

In our bathroom, the main light over the mirror gave us a chance to save even more. For quite some time — for years, actually — we had a huge light fixture up there that took eight standard incandescent bulbs. *Eight!* Even when we went down to using just 25-watt bulbs in the frumious beast, we were using 200 watts of power every time we turned it on. It was insane. It was much too much. I switched it out to a single standard four-foot fluorescent tube that only uses 32 watts. It's so much better. So much calmer. And, as I mentioned earlier, we also have a 5-watt CFL in that bathroom that I use most of the time anyway. CFLs are going to save you a fortune. There is no doubt about that.

These new low-energy light bulbs are not, however, without their interesting quirks. The first thing you're going to notice once you start using them is that they don't come on to full brightness right away. This can be more pronounced in cooler weather and is probably quite obvious further north where, as I understand it, there's a season called "winter." (You'll have to tell me about that some time.) Even down here in the Sunshine State, year around, these things can take a minute or so to come up to full light. After having used them for a few years, I hardly take any notice of their initial dimness, and out in the garage, I use it as a gauge for the outside temperature. How dim are they? Ah, that's how cool it is out here. Good thing it doesn't snow here. I'd need a flashlight.

Even after they are up to speed, you're going to have to get used to the new color of indoor lighting. CFLs tend to throw a cooler color, which is a nice way of saying your food's going to look a little green until you get used to it. I will tell you the truth: It was quite odd at first. It was really noticeable. It was not appetizing. It took some getting used to. We put those CFLs in the kitchen and dining room at the same time, and all of a sudden dinner looked like those faded, back-lit menu photos at the 24-hour restaurant. It tasted good, it just looked, well, green. (Ah, but going green is good, right?) Yeah, well, not if it makes you green, so to speak. We adapted.

I will say this, though: either the companies that manufacture CFLs have shifted the color of the light these things emit or we really have gotten used to the odd color shift. I don't notice it at all any more when we eat. The food looks just fine now, and still tastes great. Of course, now that I've mentioned it, you're going to be looking for it, and the green cast might not even be there any more. Or maybe it's just me. Tough to say. I'll tell you what: if, when you go to buy your CFLs, you look for the ones labeled "natural light" or "full spectrum light," you stand a better chance of getting lights that emit a more normal sort of sunlight glow. And you'll appreciate that every day, right around dinnertime. Bon appétit!

The other difference with CFLs is the amount of heat they *don't* emit. We all grew up learning very quickly to not touch the light bulb. It was hot. The larger ones were *very* hot. Ouch! I honestly don't think you'd want to try to unscrew a lit 25-watt incandescent bulb, now that I think about it. Even the little ones threw out some serious heat. If you live up north, this might be a good thing, as they both light and heat your home. Down here, where we've already got all the heat we want (and then some), we don't need any more, thank you very much. There's another advantage to CFLs.

These new bulbs remain quite cool to the touch. Yes, you can unscrew a lit one barehanded, if that's your idea of an exciting evening. (You're a wild thing, aren't you?) Better still, these (literally) cool new bulbs do not work against your home air conditioner, heating up the air the air conditioner just cooled. Whew. That means these silly little electric twisties are going to save you even more money in the warmer months, as your AC unit won't be working so hard to overcome the heat of all of those lamps. Go team!

The only small downside to cooler light bulbs might come when you try to use them as sort of spot dryers, like mini heat lamps. (Relax, we all do it. Or used to.) These CFLs don't do that. There's no reason to put one right over that small wet spot on your shirt, hoping you can dry it and wear it in a few minutes. Not going to happen. It will still be wet. These new CFLs don't help dry the glue on craft projects either, and are lousy for drying paint. Still, overall, they aren't a complete waste, and their inherent coolness does come with that nice economic side effect. They help you keep your cool.

As I mentioned earlier, when JoAnn and I first started switching out our old incandescent light bulbs for these new-fangled CFLs, we didn't have much to choose from. Most stores stocked just one or two different sizes, if that. Take it or leave it. We took it when we could and bought what was available, but over time, the size and variety of these new CFL bulbs became truly astounding. Now, you can get just about anything, including yellow outdoor lights, mini lights and decorative bulbs. The variety expands every year. And they are not all electric twisties any more.

One thing we have done, over time, was to go back and change out the old, higher-wattage CFLs for the newer lower-wattage CFL bulbs. I suspect the manufacturers are figuring out how to get more lumens out of fewer watts, as these new bulbs, despite their lower wattage, are really quite bright. Even a 5-watt CFL (*just five watts!*) puts out an amazing amount of light. As we switch these out, we're saving far more than we were saving the first time around. Life just keeps getting better. And smaller. And smaller is better. Whew.

Meanwhile, out beyond the breakers, we're seeing a glimpse and bright blue glimmer of the future of home lighting headed right for us (albeit slowly right now). Just as some of you have had to buy your Beatles albums time and time again as each new innovation in audio was offered to an eager, waiting public, it's starting to look as though we'll be buying all new light bulbs for our house in the years ahead. The TLT (the latest thing) is LED (light-emitting diode).

I've been using battery-powered LED lights on my bicycle for some years now, and they work great. They use very little power, emit a very bright light, and are shock proof. (They've seen it all.) These are all good things on a bicycle when you're commuting to work every day, and all six of my lights (three head lights and three taillights) use LED technology exclusively. But LEDs for the home? This is all new stuff. Welcome to the future of home lighting.

Why drop CFLs for LEDs ASAP? (Well, when you go to re-place the failed bulbs, anyway.) The math for LED home lighting is impressive. Because of their design and technology, LEDs last up to 30 times longer than those nasty, antique incandescent bulbs. They last six times longer than modern CFLs (which last a long, long time). LEDs can be good for up to 30,000 hours of use. That's a long time. You might forget how to screw in a light bulb. No joke.

They give off eight times the lumens per watt as those quaint incandescent bulbs that no one buys any more anyway, making them twice as efficient as CFLs. How does that translate to the real world? Like this: if you had an old 60-watt incandescent bulb and you wanted the same amount of light with a CFL, you put in a 15-watt CFL (one quarter the wattage). Now, with this new LED lighting technology, your next light bulb will use only 7½ watts (half of what the CFL uses). Talk about living small! Woo-hoo!

These new LEDs have other advantages as well. They put off even less heat than CFLs, which were already fairly cool, so these new LED lights will put even less of a strain on your home air conditioning system in the summer. Those vintage incandescent bulbs were really very bad about that. These new LEDs also are less likely to fail in applications where you're turning that light on and off frequently. Rumor has it CFLs are prone to that sort of failure (although, in all honesty, I've never noticed that problem with them in our house). You can also get LEDs in different brilliant colors, to give your house that home disco look, should you be the sort to go in for that kind of thing. As for me, not so much. I will say this, though: when you buy LEDs, make sure that they are labeled as "warm white" or something to that effect, to avoid their natural tendency to have a sort of bright techno-blue cast to them. That can make the room appear stark and uninviting. Fair warning there.

The thing is, however, that as I write this (early May 2008), home LEDs are, at the very least, uncommon. They are as rare as CFLs were when they first came out. It's going to take time to see this new technology in home lighting filter out to the masses (us). This should be the point in the book where I tell you that I went out and bought several new LED lights for my home last week, replaced a few CFLs with LEDs and enjoyed the new brighter lights and lower power bill. Yep, this is right where that should be. But it's not, as you can see. JoAnn and I tried both big box hardware stores in our area and got blank looks at both. We did see one LED light for home use at the local "Living Green Expo" last weekend. The lighting company that had it in their display paid $80 for it. So these spiffy new lights aren't ready to come home with you just yet. Not by a long shot at that price. The time will come when you can get them at your local grocery store, for a reasonable price, just as you can get CFLs there now. But not yet, obviously. Maybe by the time this book comes out, home LED lighting will be both available and affordable. One can only hope. I sure do.

Now I have to tell you that I do appreciate the ability to walk into any room, flip a simple switch, and have instant light at my beck and call. It really does beat dragging my knuckles into the dark cave and trying to light a woolly-mammoth-fat wax candle with a piece of flint so I can watch the latest cave drawings. It must. Still, for me, the one thing that defines civilization in my world is a hot shower. Not tepid, not warm, but mirror-steaming, lobster-poaching hot. No hot water? Then it's not really civilization, now, is it? So you can imagine my great happiness went I went to take a shower a few weeks ago and had naught but cold water. Oh, bother. After a quick dry-off, I slung on the bathrobe and went for a trot out to the library to say hello to our hot water tank and see what the problem might be. Maybe I could negotiate.

Our house was built in 1957, and for the first 35 years or so, it had a huge 50-gallon (about 230-liter) water heater. When that big boy finally gave out, we put in a more sensible 30-gallon (about 140-liter) tank. Remember: it's just JoAnn and I. I cleared away the bookcase and had a look at the water tank. Hadn't seen it for years. It was like an old friend I didn't remember ever meeting. It was also all rusty and nasty and yucky and seeping. It was definitely time for a new old friend. It was my lucky day: it was a chance to improve our water heater's efficiency and lower our monthly power bill at the expense of our Visa balance. Oh, for joy. Whoop-de-doo.

I guess that's how you have to look at it. It makes no sense to replace a perfectly good major appliance, even if you know you'll save energy and money with the new one. It is a big expense, and not something you'd want to do on a whim. No need to run right out and buy a new whatever until you absolutely have to, right? But when you do, be sure and buy a more efficient one every time. It was our time. Oh, and the little grey box timer was off. That's why I didn't have any hot water. Oops.

Remember the old bumper sticker that said, "Save water, shower with a friend!"? Yeah, well, here's the honest truth: it's a great idea, honestly, but it doesn't really save any water. You're going to be in there twice as long. Maybe longer. (Probably longer.) Odds are you're going to run out of hot water before you're ready to get out, even with a massive 50-gallon tank. Trust your Uncle Chippie on this one.

A far better idea is to get a smaller water tank that is more efficient about heating the cool incoming water in the first place. Since the 30-gallon tanks use the same heating elements as the 50-gallon tanks, I figure they heat the water faster and shut off sooner, saving you energy and money. (They have so much less to heat.) Newer tanks have much better insulation than the old

Love that little grey box!

tanks, so these new water heaters hold the water hotter longer. How good are they at that? You'll be amazed.

In addition to having just a 30-gallon water heater, we have ours on a grey box timer. Yes, the small timer does run 24/7 (nag, nag, nag), but it uses very little power compared to the water heater itself if we had simply left it running all day and night. I installed and wired the timer myself (and it hasn't caught fire yet), and it only heats the water from 5 PM to 10 PM each day. Just those five hours of power give us plenty of hot water to wash the dishes after dinner, for me to shower later that evening, and for JoAnn to take a shower the following morning after her walk (more than 10 hours after the water heater itself has shut off). Not bad. Not bad at all. That's some mighty fine insulation there.

Yes, if your home is set up for it, it would be much easier and save even more power if you simply turned the water heater off at the circuit breaker and gave yourself just 30 minutes or so before you needed that hot water to let the system heat it all up. Our house is not set up that way. In fact, we still have old-fashioned fuses. (How quaint.) It would be a real pain for us to do it that way, so the timer works well for us. Maybe some day we'll replace all of those fuses with circuit breakers. Don't hold your breath on that one.

The other thing you can do to easily lower your power bill when it comes to hot water is to adjust your water heater by lowering the thermostat. I know I said I like my showers hot, and I do, but even with the water heater's thermostat set at the lowest setting, I have plenty of hot water to keep me happy. On our new water heater, the thermostat is behind the upper removable plate. Two screws, and it was off, and all I had to do was remove a square of insulation and turn the little dial down to 90°F or 32°C

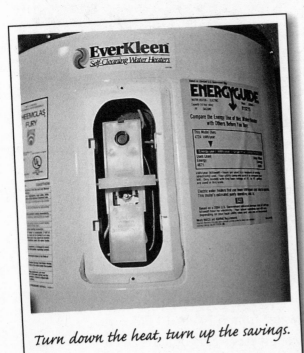

Turn down the heat, turn up the savings.

(the lowest setting on this tank). Please turn the power to the water heater off when you do this, just to be safe. I do expect to see a lower power bill next month as a result of switching to a better-insulated tank and the new low setting. (I think the old one was set at 120°F or 49°C.) I thought about monkeying around with the grey box timer while I was at it, but it works out so well for us as it is, giving the water a chance to heat up again at night after my shower (and before it shuts off) to give JoAnn plenty of hot water for hers the next morning. Let's keep everyone happy, shall we?

When it comes to heating your home's water, there's a new option on the market these days: tankless (instant-on) hot water systems. Of course it's a tankless job, but someone has to do it. (Sorry. Couldn't resist.) Now that I've got *that* out of my system, let me tell you that I did look into this spiffy new tankless hot water system when I replaced our traditional water heater (with another traditional water heater), but it wasn't for us.

There are several advantages to a tankless system. They don't heat the water until you need it, so they aren't running constantly. And that's good. Since they don't have a tank, that tank they don't have can't leak. And that's very good. And, lacking that big storage tank, they can be quite small, allowing you to put them wherever they are needed, rather than have one big tank on the far side of the house, forcing you to wait forever for hot water to reach where you are. Again, this is mostly a good thing. However (and you knew there would be a "however," didn't you?), they are not all sweetness and light. There can be issues with a tankless system.

Issue number one: tankless water heaters are not cheap. It would have cost us about twice as much to buy and install a tankless system as it did to get the classic water tank we have always had, and now have again anew. Considering how little hot water we actually use, that made the payback time very, very long indeed. Maybe too long. Even tankless systems don't last forever. And how much are those high-powered heating elements when they need to be replaced, anyway? You might want to ask about that before you buy.

Those high-powered electric heating coils were the main drawback for us. Our house couldn't handle them. The salesman at the plumbing company told us we would need to dedicate two 40-amp circuit breakers to run the tankless system, and we don't even *have* circuit breakers. (Just old fashioned fuses, remember?) So it was a total no-go for us. The power draw when the tankless system kicks on is big, and here we are trying to live small. I was told the tankless system works much better with gas heat (that avoids the big power draw when it kicks on), but we live in an all-electric home. I'd say you might want to look into it if you have gas, but then again, with the rising price of natural gas these days, maybe not. We've got what we've got, and it works well for us, thanks to that little grey box timer and the lowered thermostat setting (and the increased thermal efficiency of these new hot water tanks). We're still living small and showering hot. Civilization is a good thing.

Another option that I know you're probably wondering about (and you should be) is solar water heating. We live in Florida, the Sunshine State, so you'd think that solar would be the obvious answer for water heating and power, right? Maybe, maybe not. Not for us, anyway. Yes, many homes down here, especially those with swimming pools, use huge black mats on their roofs to heat water using only the power of the sun. And, yes, that's a very good way to do it around here. For us, however, it would be a step backward. It would be counterproductive. We have something better than the sun. We have shade.

Specifically, we have a lot of big trees all around our house, and those big trees keep our home shady and cool, protected from that relentless Florida sun. Yes, it does get warm down here, but not in the shade. Keeping our house cool is, to me, more important than heating up a little bit of water. That precious shade allows us to be less dependent on our energy-intensive air conditioning. If we wanted to install a solar water heater on the roof, we'd have to cut back quite a few of the tree limbs that shade our entire house, intentionally exposing the roof to the hot Florida sun and then installing a big black panel of tubes full of hot water that would heat the roof, and our house, even more. That doesn't sound like living small to me.

My approach to low-energy living involves — and brace yourself here — actually using less, not more. For me, getting by with no technology at all trumps having to buy any technology at all, even low technology. If I keep my home covered with natural shade, that does preclude the use of a solar water heating system, but the house stays so cool the overall energy savings are worth it. Yes, I could go all high-tech with a solar water heating system, but that's not me. I'm a low-tech kind of guy. Ask anyone. (And, yes, the irony of typing those words on a computer is not entirely lost on me.)

One place where the sun really can help you out is in drying your clothes. Yes, we have a big, honking 220-volt electric clothes dryer, but it's not a bad idea to supplement that energy-intensive hot tumbler with a simple clothesline in the back yard. What could be easier than that? Until the sun starts sending out

An energy-saving blast from the past

monthly bills, this could be the way to go, or at least help out
a bit.

No, you don't have to dry all of your clothes on a clothesline.
The neighbors don't need to see your boxers and briefs, and you
needn't mention your unmentionables to anyone. Then again, if
you want to save energy and money on washday, it might not
hurt to have a portable clothesline you can set up just on washday. Do the heavy pants and shirts first (and maybe the towels),
then string them up to dry in the sun while you do the lighter
stuff you can throw in the dryer for a much shorter amount of
time. If you cut your dryer use in half, you're going to save the

cost of that clothesline in fairly short order. At 220 volts to power a big clothes dryer, those savings are going to show up quick on your monthly power bill.

And, yes, this is going to be one of the rare times when I tell you to go out and buy something to save energy and money in the long run. A portable (collapsible) clothesline, a bag of clothespins, and a plastic pipe to sink in the ground to hold it up is, all told, a small investment and, I think, money well spent. (Don't forget the cap for the plastic pipe to keep rain water out of it.) Want to go a little crazy with it? Get one of those little concrete rings that go around a sprinkler head to protect the pipe in the ground when you mow.

Drawbacks to a clothesline? There are a few. Primarily, you have to be comfortable with hanging your clothes out on a line for all to see. I have no problem with that, but, yes, the undies go in the dryer, thanks for asking. Humble humility aside, the other thing you might want to check on is any neighborhood or city deed restriction that would prohibit the use of a clothesline, if you live someplace that has restrictions on what you can do in and around your own home. I don't. (Lucky me!) It is true that some places don't allow clotheslines. These are places I don't want to live, but you might be stuck there. My sympathy. All you can do is hope to change the rules. Good luck with that. My wonderful wife does tell me that in some places, municipal regulations in favor of clotheslines trump private development deed restrictions against them. So there you go.

Other than humility and maybe deed restrictions, all it takes is a little bit of effort and nice weather on washday to put up a clothesline for the day. Wash the heavy stuff first, and enjoy the savings when the power bill comes in. Seems like a small price to pay to live a little smaller. Of course, this means it'll rain on washday. Never fails.

Now how about we drag the sun-dried hats off of our heads for a rare moment of silence in honor of Philo T. Farnsworth (1906–1971)? Young Philo, at a very tender age, invented the television as we know it today. I guess he really didn't want to do his homework. These days, the flickering blue light of the television seems to be the one constant in every home. Walk around your neighborhood at night and you will see that the TV is everyone's night-light. With very few exceptions, we all watch TV. Yes, even me. The thing is, with all of those TVs on all the time, there has to be a way to use less power. I mean, short of just turning the silly thing off.

The first problem we're up against when it comes to efficient television use is the sad fact that all of these new, larger flat-screen TVs use a tremendous amount of power. Far, far more than the old cathode ray tube (CRT) models we've all used for years. As I look around at the new TVs on the market these days, I'm not even sure you could go out and buy a new CRT model TV anywhere any more. Are we stuck with using more power for no good reason? So it would seem. Is there any way to use less power? Maybe. Sort of.

Obviously, the first option is also the least likely: turn the thing off. Could you stand to watch a little less TV? I think we all could, but far be it from me to tell you to do that. You like your shows and I like mine. That's why there are 57 channels and, in the words of The Boss, ain't nothing on. Still, someone must be watching all that stuff, and they're all using power to do so. Could you skip one show a week that you watch these days? How about one less show per day? Every little bit helps, and watching less TV might be a better thing for all of us. It's a chance I'm willing to take. Who's with me on this? Anyone? Anyone? Oh, well. It was worth a try. Where's the remote?

I suspect you're holding out for a viable Plan B. You want your MTV, but you'd like to save some money as well. Fine. I can work with that. I have the answer, and JoAnn and I have been using it for years: the ubiquitous power strip. (If yours isn't ubiquitous, don't worry, just about any power strip will do.) The problem with your television is the problem with virtually all electronics: even if you turn them off, they still use power. It's crazy. This weird phantom power drain shows up in your power bill every month, driving you nuts if you're trying to lower that bill and you have no idea where it's all going (and why you're having to pay for it). It's all going right down the drain while you're not looking. It has to stop, and it can if you use a power strip.

This is so easy: Plug the power strip into the wall outlet. Now plug your TV, cable box, VCR, DVD and anything else within reach into that plugged-in power strip. Everything plugged into the strip? Great. You're done. Now all you do is turn the power strip on when you want to watch TV, and (here's the important part) turn the power strip *off* when you're done. Now, when the power strip is off, all of those power-draining electronics are truly *off* and dead, and not just using power quietly without telling you. You have control. You have, quite literally, the power. Use it wisely, my young apprentice.

The key to success with this idea is for you to always remember to turn the power strip off. It can be easy to forget. Real easy. Any time you're not watching the tube, that strip should be off. At night when you're asleep, while you're at work during the day, or whenever you're out of the house, for whatever reason, there's no reason on earth for all of that equipment to sit there busting electrons for no good reason. Except...

Except when you want to tape something that comes on when you're asleep, at work, or otherwise not there. Then, yes, you do have to let the beast breathe. C'est la vie. The funny thing is, you have no idea how many times we've carefully set up all of the equipment to record some obscure, must-see late-night TV show, only to immediately shut it all off with the power strip and blissfully go off to bed. Oops. These things happen. But at least we remembered to turn it all off!

For all of you audiophiles out there, the same philosophy must certainly apply to whatever sound equipment you have on that shelf in the rumpus room, constantly seething electrons whether it's making any noise or not. No matter what the system, no matter what the format, turn it off when it's not in use. Put everything on a power strip and turn the power strip off. Then unplug the power strip from the wall, just to make sure. (I'm kidding.) (Sort of.) The same can be said for your home computer. As if it was ever not in use.

The home computer is a wonderful thing. You can use it to store your favorite recipes and all of your mailing addresses, exchange messages with far-flung friends, and catch up on the news. You can do with it pretty much everything we all used to do with a pencil and paper. Great thing, the computer. The drawback? Well, unlike the pencil and paper, and much like the TV, the computer uses a lot of power, even just sitting there. It can be worse than your TV in that regard.

Look at your home computer system: you have a monitor (just another word for TV), the hard drive, keyboard, mouse, scanner, printer and audio/video system, all wired together and all using power. Yes, it's a wonderful thing, but that wonderful thing could be costing you energy and money every minute of every day, whether you're seriously surfing or not. And it's the "not" that sneaks up and bites you on that monthly power bill.

As with everything electronic, it's often not enough to just hit the power switch and assume that it's off. "Off" is a funny word and means many things to many people. To electronics people, "off" means "almost on." And "almost on" is going to cost you. Hard drives and monitors also generate a little bit of heat (admittedly not much), so there's also that aspect of the computer equipment working against the air conditioning, but that's certainly not the big issue here. It's all about squelching the constant standby power drain. It's about "off" really meaning "off." If you want "off" to mean "off" (and to *be* "off"), then it's up to you to make it so. Just as with the TV and audio equipment, plug your entire computer system into a power strip, and when you aren't using it, turn the power strip off. Saving energy (and saving money) is that simple and yet so few people do it. Be a pioneer. Turn your stuff off. All of it. Every time. Thank you.

Those pesky phantom power drains are all over the place in most homes. Every electronic toy that uses a battery charging station is using a little bit of power, sometimes 24/7. Even if we're only talking a single watt or so for each item, they all add up when they're just sitting there plugged in all of the time. Some small thing that uses just a single watt of power, 24 hours a day, uses almost ¾ of a kilowatt (730 watts) in a single month's time. That's almost nine kilowatts a year, and you're paying for it every month.

Someone once told me that our doorbell was a phantom power drain. *Huh?* Were they joking? They were serious. I looked into it, and all I can figure is this: if you have one of those doorbells where the outside push button actually lights up, then, yes, it is using power 24/7. No, it's not using much power, but it goes back to the one-watt-every-hour thing. One watt at a time does add up, and over, say, a year's time, that lit-up doorbell uses a surprising amount of power. Our doorbell button does not light up. Problem solved right there before it was a problem.

Your cell phone, handheld electronic organizer, pager, you name it — even though they are battery-powered, those batteries get their power from your home 110-volt system. And power costs. Absolute power costs absolutely. You see it every month in your electric bill. You pay for it every month. How much would you save if you unplugged all of the chargers around your home except when you needed them to charge the item in question? Let's find out. Search out every last one of them and unplug them. Plug them in only for the short amount of time needed to charge the thing, then make sure you unplug them again. You're not going to be able to put the dog through college with the savings (well, maybe a two-year college), but you will save a pile of coins in a year's time. And every coin counts. Even the little ones. Watch every watt every minute. Your local power company might not thank you, but your wallet will. As do I.

5

Living Small *and* Keeping Your Cool

NOW IT'S TIME TO STEP BACK and take in the big picture: the house, the whole house, and nothing but the house. We're talking about my house, your house, and the houses we are both mostly stuck with. There are a lot of things we can both change around our houses and in our houses to use less energy and live small, but the house itself? We're both kind of stuck there, aren't we?

I lucked out. I live in the house my parents bought when we all moved to Florida many years ago, and it's a good house. For using less energy, it's a great house, and that has nothing to do with anything I've done. It's all about how the house was built, where the house was built, and the building's orientation when it comes to the prevailing wind. It is, as they say, all about location, location, location. And even though there's not a thing you can do about it (short of picking the house up and moving it), it doesn't hurt to check around and find out about the prevailing winds where you live, just in case you might be able to make

Gotta love all those trees!

use of them. At least it will give you some idea of what you're up against.

In my part of the world (west central Florida), the prevailing winds come either from the north or from the south. To take advantage of those cooling breezes, you want a home that is built longer along its east-west axis, giving the dominant winds more of a chance to blow through a larger portion of your home if you open the windows. Our home is all of that and more. Not only is our house primarily an east-west structure, the living room has massive floor-to-ceiling windows on both sides of it (looking out over both the front yard and the back yard) that allow a breeze to go right through entire house. Now that's cool!

The dominant window style down here, for a house of this age (about 50 years old) is something called a "Miami" window. These are windows that are glass panels framed in aluminum and hinged at the top of each panel so that each whole window is made up of a number of panels that all swivel out on hinges operated by a hand crank inside the house. The big advantage to a Miami window is that, when it is open, it is *entirely* open. Every inch of it allows a breeze to pass through into the house. Also, unless the wind is really howling, you can leave them open when it rains, and nothing inside gets wet. Well, not usually. Except for our kitchen and bathroom windows, all of the windows in the main part of our home are Miami windows. It can be quite the wind tunnel, and those big windows keep the house amazingly cool in the summer. This house is saving us a fortune.

By comparison, single-hung or double-hung windows (we have single-hung windows in the bathrooms and kitchen) only allow you to open half of the window to allow a breeze to enter the home. They do seal more tightly when closed, but you pay for that with far less ventilation. At the other end of the window spectrum are jalousie or louvered windows. (Or as we call them, jealousy windows, as they have to be jealous of real windows.) These windows are made up

Miami windows keep us cool.

of many narrow strips of glass with no metal frame at all, and hinge and open much like Miami windows, but seal when closed much like a pitchfork. Which is to say, not at all. We had these windows in both bathrooms, the kitchen and the door to the garage, but changed them out some years ago for real windows that actually closed. We still have them in the adventure room at the back of the house. They make Miami windows look like a good idea. Jalousie windows are truly abysmal.

You have to understand that, living in Florida as I do, I'm mostly concerned with keeping cool in the summer. We only have three seasons down here — spring, summer and fall — but since we give winter a miss, each season we do have lasts four months instead of three. A small price to pay, I think. So, with no winter, I'm all about keeping the house cool using the least amount of energy possible, especially in the summer (June through September). In that regard, I think we're doing quite well down here. And I haven't had to shovel snow in almost 40 years. Go team.

Even though much of what I'm going to say about energy savings regarding the home itself is going to be about saving electricity (we have central air conditioning and electric heat), this section on the home gets its own chapter anyway. Much of what we have done around the home to use less energy has been "unpowered" changes that use no electricity at all. They are inert, physical changes that, once done, are done. No power required. We've done a lot over the years, but some things were done before we ever moved into the house and some of what was done was done when the house was built, by someone who really knew what he (or she) was doing. As I mentioned earlier, we lucked out with this house.

And, yes, the whole idea of keeping cool or warm can be quite subjective. What I find tolerable for a temperature in my house might drive you crazy. Life's funny that way. Are you old enough to remember Jimmy Carter in a cardigan? (You don't have to admit it, just nod quietly to yourself.) During the energy crisis of the late 1970s, President Carter told us to set the thermostat to 68°F (20°C) in the winter and 78°F (25½°C) in the summer. He wore a sweater indoors in the winter. He put solar panels on the White House roof. Say what you want about the man (and many do), but he understood what we were up against long before anyone else knew there was any problem at all. Reagan had those solar panels off the White House roof faster than a bad taffeta prom dress. Go figure.

These days, for me, 78° (25½°) in the house is cool and comfortable. Our house is usually much cooler than that inside without using air conditioning. (And did I mention we live in Florida?) I do believe people can adapt, somewhat, to wherever they are. I'm used to living here in the heat and humidity, but I've lived here for almost 40 years. You might not fare so well here if you were to simply show up unannounced in August. You might find it a tad, well, sticky. "Close," as they say here in the South.

One thing you can do, wherever you live, is to make small changes over time. If you've been running your home air conditioning at 72° (22°), try 74° (23¼°). Get used to that. Give it a couple of weeks, and then try 76° (24½°). Small changes over time. Baby steps. If you take the first half of the summer to adapt to 78° (25½°) in your house, you're going to save a bundle of money over the second half of the summer with your air conditioning set at that new higher temperature. Just promise yourself you'll start next summer at 78° (25½°), and think of the savings!

The same must be true for adapting to a cooler indoor temperature up north in the winter. Making incremental changes in the heat, lowering it just a couple of degrees over time, will help you get used to it. Well, that and a good cardigan. You also have to dress for the climate wherever you live. If you live where it's cold, you have to dress for the cold. If you live where it's warm, you dress for it. I sure do. (You should see my extensive collection of tropical shirts!) I wouldn't try to go north and dress as I do down here. I'd freeze. In the summer, you dress for the summer. Just as President Carter wore a cardigan in the winter, dressing for the season will help save you energy and money year around. And hey, you look good in that sweater. Honestly.

For me, here in Florida, virtually 100 percent of my effort to keep my house comfortable is in keeping my house cool. For us, down here, that usually means keeping the sun out as much as possible. And as much as I hate grey, overcast days (and I really do), I have to admit, I really don't spend much time out basking in the direct sun. I'm more of a deep shade type of guy. The deep shade keeps both me and my house happy.

Around my house, shade means trees. Our home is on a third of an acre corner lot, and we have 15 trees on that lot and still have room for the house. (The house takes up about 2,000 square feet (185 m²), including the garage.) We have some huge oak trees in our yard, and, along with all of the other trees, that means the roof of our house is protected from direct sun all day. The result? Our house stays amazingly cool on the warmest day. That's why I won't cut these wonderful trees down to put up any sort of high-tech solar system to heat water, generate electricity, or whatever. It would be counter-productive. It would cost me. These trees are saving me more money than I could hope to gain with any increased technology that would cost me the trees and that glorious shade.

Several of the large oak trees closest to our house had to have been on this land long before the house was built. They're huge. Whoever built our house was smart to nestle this home in among what were, even 50 years ago, some big shady trees. I've planted additional trees over the years and watched them grow to where they add their fair share of shade as well. The moral of the story? Plant trees. Plant many, many trees, all around your house. They will shade your house in the summer and break the cold wind in the winter. They give you birds to watch, squirrels to laugh at, and big gnarly roots to whack the snot out of your lawn mower blade. They'll keep you on your toes. Mostly, though, they are very good for lowering your home's energy needs (and they look great). Want another reason to plant trees? With all of the big shade trees around this house, our home is virtually invisible from the air. I kind of like that. Take that, Google Earth!

Another thing that helps us keep the sun out of our house is something you probably wouldn't want north at

Wide eaves make for great shade.

all: wide eaves. Ours are huge. They are over two feet wide, and run all around the house. (Our single-story house was built with a hip roof and has no gables at all.) This puts our east-facing windows in the shade much sooner as the sun comes up, and holds the shade over our single west-facing window longer in the afternoon. Like I said, someone really thought this one out when they built this house as they put the garage on the west side of the house to help block the living area from the warmer, lingering afternoon sun.

I know there's not much you can do about the depth of your house's eaves after the house is built, but you can add awnings over the windows to help shade the interior. This is more crucial over the south and west windows that get more sun. If you don't have trees, awnings are a quick way to make shade while you plant trees and wait for them to grow. Trees are not notoriously quick in that regard. Patience, Grasshopper.

Down here in the Danger Zone, we also see a lot of homes with big metal (aluminum) awnings that can be brought down over the windows they shade as protective hurricane shutters. Correctly sized and installed, they are, I think, a great idea. You get the use of the shutter as shade, and the use of the shade as a shutter. We also see canvas window awnings down here, but they make lousy shutters when there's a big storm rolling in. Great for shade, though! Go with the aluminum awnings/shutters if you live south of I-10 or anywhere near the Gulf or Atlantic coast. Be safe. That's important, too.

There are also things you can do from inside your house to help use less energy. To keep your home cool in the summer, reflective solar film on the windows is an obvious choice here in Florida, but that might not be your best choice if you live up north. For me, here, it's all about keeping our house cool in the endless summer. Further north (north of, say, that infamous I-10), you're fighting the energy battle on two fronts, trying to use less energy to keep cool in the summer, but also trying to use less energy to keep warm in the winter. For you, that reflective solar film on all of those windows is a bad idea, as the film will block the much-needed warming rays of the sun in the winter, when you really could use them to help keep your house warm. So, in the words of Bugs Bunny: it's curtains for you. Aw, aren't they nice?

If your home is lacking eaves and awnings and needs to both reflect and absorb sunshine as the seasons change, your best bet might be to have two sets of curtains. Light-colored curtains for the summer months will help reflect sunlight coming in the windows and keep your rooms cool. Light-colored thermal curtains will do even better to keep the heat down. Just the thing for those bright, sunny days in the warm summer months.

In the winter, you'll want to switch to darker curtains to help convert direct sunlight to heat at every window. Again, thermal curtains aren't a bad idea to help hold the house's heat in at night. If you can open the curtains on the south side of the house in the winter to get direct sunlight into your home, you'll notice a big difference in the temperature in those south-facing rooms. The sun is a powerful energy source, even up north in the winter. You will have to keep an eye on it all, though, and as the sun moves and the direct sunlight goes away, it's time to close those curtains for the day.

For us, in our house, we work hard to keep our windows open in the summer, to keep those cool breezes flowing through. Yes, we button it all up tighter than a drum if we go away, but if we're there, that home is a breezy collection of open windows. We live just 2½ miles from the Gulf of Mexico *and* Tampa Bay (right between the two), so it seems as though there's always a breeze blowing in from somewhere. If we're lucky, it blows right through the house and keeps us cool on its way to somewhere else. Just passing through? Cool.

Oh, and, yes, over the years, we have learned to arrange whatever small things we have in the house so they won't blow over if the breeze picks up suddenly, as it has been known to do in Florida from time to time (nudge, nudge, wink, wink). It's not as though we glue every object in the house to the shelf it's on, but the light stuff is usually kept away from the windows (and down low). Nevertheless, I'll bet that about once a year or so we're woken up in the middle of the night by the sound of something being blown over somewhere in the house as the breeze picks up unexpectedly. The game is to then guess what it was *before* you go look. What fun! Now where's the broom?

But what if you don't live in sunny Florida, where the weather's always lovely and the oranges grow on trees? What if you live up north, where it can get a bit nippy (or so I've heard)? I was going to tell you it's not my area of expertise, but, truth be told, I have lived where it's cold. In some ways, it's not so different. More often than not, staying warm and staying cool (and using less energy to do so) are both about working with the sun and the judicious application of insulation. In either case, it's simply not possible to have too much insulation.

What we have done down here to stay cool, you do up north to stay warm: put as much insulation as possible in the attic and rafters. Insulation under the house, if possible. (Ours is on slab, so it's not). Insulation in the walls, and most certainly around

Now that's some insulation. What's in your attic?

the windows and doors. Where we want cooling breezes down south in the summer, you want no breezes whatsoever up north in the winter. You do not want to have to calculate the wind chill factor *inside* your house. Nobody wants that.

If you live where it gets cold, start with sealing your outer doors. They should seal as tightly as possible when closed. If this means adding extra weather stripping to seal any gaps, that's time and money well spent to save energy and money all winter. Know what a draft dodger is? No, it's a heavy roll of cloth that lies against the inside bottom of an outer door to stop the cool air from seeping through. Not a bad thing to have for every outer door. Make sure those outer doors are sealed tightly. Much of the same can be said for your windows.

Make sure all of your windows close and seal as tightly as they can. I know that sounds screamingly obvious, but it's amazing how often windows don't really seal very tightly at all, and you can feel the air whistling in around them. You do not want that in the winter. The snow should stay on the outside, no matter how picture-postcard-perfect it is. On top of that, you can (and should) add storm windows to the outside of the house to add a layer of trapped air insulation at every window. Trapped air, especially where it can be heated by the sun, is an excellent way to help keep your house warm and your power bill low. Storm doors work just as well outside your regular doors to add a layer of warmed air there, too. Make sure you have both, and use them throughout the winter.

One long-standing clever trick is to seal the house up as tightly as you can for the winter and light a candle in the middle of every room. (Not all at once, mind you. One room at a time, so you can keep an eye on it.) If that candle flame flickers at all, in any way, you've got a draft somewhere. You can move the candle closer to the windows and doors and watch to see where it moves even more. There's your problem, right there. Until the flame is unmoved, the room is not yet sealed, and you're losing heat somewhere. Try to not breathe on it. That tends to screw up the readings, so to speak.

Want to lose a lot of hot air fast? That's easy: just leave your fireplace flue open when you don't have a fire in the fireplace. Warm air rises (that's why the chimney works in the first place), and the warm air will rise right out of your house and straight up the chimney. Or is it the heavier cold air that comes down into the house? It doesn't matter. Either way: if there is no fire, close the flue! We have a nice little brick fireplace in our adventure room, and I have a strip of wood that I keep attached to the flue handle when I don't have a fire in the fireplace. It says, "Flue Closed," to remind me to *open* the flue before I start a fire. (Very important message, if you're me.) I keep that piece of wood handy after I've opened the flue and started the fire, so I remember, once the fire is truly out, usually the next morning, to go back in there and close the flue again. It's easy to overlook, since it's not like you can actually see whether or not the flue is open or closed. Make sure you know. Either way.

By far the best way to keep your house warmer in the winter without using excess energy and money is to do all you can to let the sun do all it can. This usually means making sure south- and west-facing windows are able to catch all the sun available. And

Always close the flue when the fire is out.

that might mean (Gasp!) trimming back trees and bushes that may block the sun from hitting those windows with direct sunlight. This is especially true of the evergreens that don't lose their leaves in the winter. If you have to, you have to. Just be gentle, and don't trim back any more than you have to. After you've done all you can to insulate your house, checked every window and door, it's all about adding sunlight to warm the house. There is, of course, the Uncle Chippie way to keep warm in the winter: move to Florida and don't look back. Ah, Paradise!

I moved to Florida in the summer of 1969, one week out of high school. I had lived in colder climates, including southeastern Ohio, along Lake Michigan north of Chicago, and in the German Alps. I've seen it snow on the fourth of July, and let me tell you, that's not nearly as funny as it sounds. The longer I stay here in Florida, the less inclined I am to leave. I've found that I don't really miss the cold at all. We have our seasons down here, just not the cold one. I can live with that.

Short of moving to Florida (and let's not rule that out entirely just yet), insulation, and lots of it, is the key to lowering your energy use and power bill, winter or summer. It works both ways, giving you what you want year around. Since hot air rises (and you want to keep it in the winter) and the sun beats down on your roof (and you want to protect the interior of your home from it in the summer), the first place you need to go overboard with insulation is up in your attic and around your rafters.

Some years ago, as we started to get far more serious about lowering our monthly electric bill, JoAnn and I had our local power company come out and do an energy inspection of our home. The inspection was free, they pointed out all the areas where we could save money, and they gave us discount certificates for having insulation blown into our attic. What a deal! Call your power company, and ask if they offer anything like this. If they do, by all means, take them up on their offer and follow through on their suggestions.

Generally speaking, you've got three main options these days when it comes to adding attic insulation. You can have loose insulation blown into the spaces between the ceiling joists, as we did. You can also have liquid expanding foam insulation blown directly onto the rafters and on the wood holding up the roof. The third option is to have insulation blocks cut and installed between the rafters, again, just under the roof. We went with the blown insulation between the ceiling joists, since there really wasn't enough room up in our attic for people to get in there to either spray the liquid expanding foam or cut and install big blocks of insulation. Admittedly, some of this you can do yourself if you're overly ambitious. We simply got the free energy inspection from the local power company, took their discount insulation offer, and wrote a check to the insulation company for the work they did. Problem solved, insulation added, power bill lowered. Life is good. Better, actually.

We did go with blown cellulose insulation, as we were told it was the better way to go. It's not at all itchy (like fiberglass), it doesn't compact over time (as our original insulation did), and it tends to keep the bugs and vermin away. Since our attic is open to the garage, and the garage door is open quite a bit (I'm out there working on bikes a lot), these were all good selling points. We have seen very few bugs around anywhere since we had that done, and, considering this is Florida, that borders on a minor miracle right there. I think we made a wise choice by going with the cellulose insulation. Our power bill thinks so, too.

There is a fourth option for insulating your attic. This is one that friends of ours did, and it worked out quite well for them. They live in a colorful cottage called the Whimzy Whimsical House in Safety Harbor, Florida, that features exposed rafters, so they really have no attic at all, but do have a loft bedroom just under the roof. To help insulate the cottage from the sun beating down on the roof, they installed hundreds of collectible metal school lunch boxes in the spaces between the rafters, just under the roof. The result is amazing: colorful, funny and surprisingly effective. Trapped air is trapped air, even when it's trapped in a vintage Happy Days metal lunch box.

In warmer weather (and certainly in warmer climates), the afternoon and evening sun bakes the west side of the house. To keep your house cooler in the summer you need to pay particular attention to the insulation on that side of the house. West-facing windows and doors need to work harder to keep that late-day heat out. Even the color of the window frame is important.

I've seen modern office buildings where the windows, as thick as they were, were held in place with dark anodized aluminum frames, and those dark window frames on the west side of the building got too hot to touch on a sunny afternoon. The dark tinted window glass itself stays cool on the inside, but heat was transferred into the building through the dark window frames, and those got brutally hot. The solution for your home? White window frames, obviously. That, alone, makes a big difference in the amount of heat coming into the home on the west side of the house. You might consider white window frames along the south side of your house as well, if those windows get direct summer sun. Every little bit helps, and white paint is relatively cheap.

For us, the big deal was the garage door. We have an 18-foot-wide garage door (about 5½ meters) that takes up almost the entire west face of our home. It's huge. For about the first 40 years of our home's life, that door was a single-panel uninsulated metal door. Galvanized steel, I think. (It was not aluminum. It was too heavy.) And, for those first 40 years or so, that door would get fried-egg hot every afternoon as the Florida sun beat down on it. Even well after sunset, you could put your hand up to the inside of that door and feel the heat radiating off it, noticeably warming the garage, just as though it needed to be. It did not.

We went through a rash of home improvement projects a while back, and up near the top of the list (right under "new roof") was "new garage door." It was time to solve the problem and keep the garage, and therefore the house, cooler. We went with a multi-panel insulated aluminum door with galvanized-steel storm ribs. What a world of difference that made! Now, no matter how hot it is outside, no matter how long the sun has been beating down on that poor, defenseless garage door, the inside of the door stays comfortable and cool, the garage stays comfortable and cool, and we stay comfortable and cool. A winning situation all around.

By the way, our garage door is not stark white. Yes, I know that would be a better color for it to reflect all of that afternoon heat, but our house is, technically, painted "Sun City", sort of a light tan. The garage door was white when we got it, but it stood out too much for our taste, so we painted it to match the house. Did it make a difference? Not really. Did the door get hotter? Maybe just a little, but not enough for us to notice.

And that new roof I just mentioned? The original white concrete tile roof lasted 40 years, but it was time for a change. (It had sprung a leak.) The new roof is fiberglass shingle, and it is a sort of medium brown. Yes, much darker than the original white roof, but with all of the insulation we have in the attic, the house still stays remarkably cool. If we had painted the old, heavy tile roof brown and not added any insulation in the attic, I don't doubt that we would have turned our home into one big Dutch oven. As it turned out, the new brown roof didn't set us back in our quest for cool.

When the new roof was installed, the roofers also installed a ridge vent along the top ridge of the roof to let the hot air in the attic escape. I think that might also help keep our home cool. It's not as though I notice a stiff breeze ripping through the garage or anything, but I have to admit our home does stay remarkably cool, even in the heat of summer. Even in Florida.

Now, should you have a stack of coins burning a hole in your pocket, better windows might be a good investment to lower your energy use and save you money in the long run. Windows last a very long time, so this might be money well spent. Double pane (do they even make triple pane?) thermal windows will help cut down on heat loss in the winter and keep your house cooler in the summer. They will also keep your house cleaner and quieter by sealing better. You will notice the difference.

JoAnn and I changed out the windows in both bathrooms and the kitchen when we did our big home improvement thing a few years ago. Those three rooms all had the infamously bad jalousie windows. They were truly horrible windows — noisy, dirty and drafty — and they all had to go. The new windows are white vinyl-framed and single-hung. Nothing extravagant, but good windows that do a great job of sealing and helping us use less energy year around. In addition, we changed out one door (the door from the dining room to the garage) that had a long, narrow jalousie window right down the middle of it. The new door has a smaller single-hung window. Much better. Yes, we're all about getting a cool breeze through the house for most of the year, but when it does get cool down here, we do want to keep the house comfortably warm. We do, after all, have orange juice for blood.

It's all about using the sun, or avoiding the sun, to keep your home comfortable year around. In the summer, you want to keep your house, especially your windows, in the shade and out of the sun. You want to be able to open up your home and invite the breeze to blow right through to keep you cool. You want trees and deep shade and plenty of insulation between you and the sun. But that's only in the summer. A few months later, the sun is your long-lost friend, and you want to invite him everywhere in your home. In the winter, direct sunlight is the cheapest heat in town, and if you can use the sun to help warm your home through the winter, you are far ahead of the game. After all, it's not as though you can just pick up your house and move it. You've got to work with what you've got, and we've all got the sun. Work with it.

Saving Water One Drop at a Time

S OME YEARS AGO I wrote a short essay entitled "The Forgotten Commodity." It was all about fresh water as the limit to human development in any one place. The limit to growth is not about roads and schools or power plants and shopping malls — it's all about water. No water? No deal. No growth. You have to have water. Without it, nothing happens.

Now, the funny thing is, the amount of water on planet earth never really changes. It can't really go anywhere else, but it does change form (ice, water or vapor), and it does migrate over time. And, yes, we can screw it up and make some of it pretty much useless for a while. We're very good at that.

Through evaporation and precipitation, water is naturally recycled all over the world. We are constantly getting new fresh water as rain, but we are also constantly using that fresh water, and often for all the wrong reasons. Even salt water evaporates to become fresh water rain, so why is fresh water such a topic of concern? It's because while the amount of water on planet earth remains the same, we are constantly making more people.

And they all get thirsty. We seem to always need more water, and that's simply not possible. Water is, after all, the limit to growth.

In our house, JoAnn pays the bills. I never see them, but do occasionally ask. I snagged an old water bill the other day and called the water department to figure out how to read our bill — that is, how to look at our water bill and figure out how much we used. Even though we live in the county, we have city water. Ironically enough, we have Clearwater city water. And, not so ironically, it tastes great. As well it should, considering. The lady who answered the phone in the City of Clearwater Water Department (April) was very nice and walked me through the bill. Water is measured in units, and each unit of water is equal to 748 gallons (2,842.4 l). Not 750 (2,850). Go figure. It must be a government thing. By multiplying the units used by 748, you get the gallons used in that billing cycle. For us, we used 2,200 gallons (8,360 l) of water last month, and it cost us $15.94. Considering the minimum billing rate is good for up to 6,700 gallons (about 25,500 l), I think we do very well when it comes to conserving water. So did April.

The question is, no matter how much water you use (or what they charge for it), can you get by with using less water? Odds are you can. Let's start inside the house, with the bathroom. That's where we use a lot of water, so maybe that's where we can save a lot of water. Shall we go ahead and start with the shower? Why not?

Since we have to (sadly) admit that showering with a friend is not, in fact, a water-saving solution, what can we do in that regard? You are going to use less water if you take a shower (alone) instead of a bath (alone), so you're on the right track already. The next thing you need to do is install a low-flow showerhead. I know, I know, it's like having a yard gnome hold a sprinkler can over your head. You get used to it.

JoAnn and I were able to snag a couple of home water use reduction kits from our local (county) utilities department that included low-flow showerheads and low-flow faucet aerators. They were easy to install. All we had to do

Low-flow looks pretty good, huh?

was screw them in place and we were good to go. Yes, the low-flow showerhead took a little getting used to, but it was nice. Very relaxing and calming. And the yard gnome was polite.

If you want a quicker way to reduce water use, simply install stainless steel washers behind the showerhead and faucet aerator. Same result: less water comes out. Just make sure they are stainless steel washers, unless you have a serious iron deficiency and really need more rusty water.

I might also put in a word here about being snappy about it. (In the shower, that is.) It's very easy to take a long, relaxing shower, and even with that new low-flow showerhead, you can use up far more water than you ever did before. So step it up a bit, why don't you? People are waiting! Chop, chop! Sorry. Someone had to tell you.

If you're really serious about saving water when you shower, there's always "the Navy way." As I understand it, the Navy way is to turn on the shower only long enough to get wet, then turn the shower completely off. You lather up while the shower is off, and turn it back on again to rinse off. Yes, this would save some water (I guess), but the annoyance factor goes up a notch or two as well. Is it worth it? Not if you don't like it. I want my green routine to be a pleasant and enjoyable experience. Standing in a cold shower stall covered in soap is not all that pleasant. I prefer to work fast and keep the water flowing.

Noses and faucets should not run.

Meanwhile, outside the shower, I never did notice a difference with those low-flow faucet aerators we installed. Everything worked just fine before, and everything works just fine now. I honestly can't tell the difference. (Did I accidentally put the originals back on, I wonder?) With these faucets, whether in the bathroom, the kitchen, or wherever, the key to using less water could not possibly be simpler: just turn it off!

Whenever I'm washing my hands, brushing my teeth or shaving, I don't let the water just run. I run it when I need it and shut it off when I don't. (Yes, it's sort of like the Navy shower, but without ending up covered head to toe in soap.) I know this sounds picky and petty and annoying, but it really does help. (And it's nowhere near as annoying as the Navy shower.) (By the way, can you tell I'm an old *Army* brat?) You will use a lot less water if you get into the habit of turning off the tap when you don't need it. Yes, it does take a bit more effort to keep turning it off and on, so, yes, it might take you slightly longer to do whatever it is you're doing with all of that water, but — it's worth it. You will use less water, and that's the whole idea of living small and going green. Good for you.

Now we're going to have to talk about a somewhat, um, sensitive subject: the toilet. Your toilet. (Because we sure aren't going to talk about my toilet.) This is one place where we all use a lot of water every day, and maybe we could use a little less (without getting all icky about it).

Remember the old idea of putting a brick in your toilet tank to use less water? As it turns out, that brick dissolves over time, thanks to the constant emersion in water. Probably not a good idea. These days, the thing is to use a water dam or a small plastic jug or bottle full of water, weighted to hold it in place (small rocks work great), to help displace water that might otherwise go out with every flush. Then again, you might not need to do anything at all.

If your toilet is one of the new low-flow models, it uses only about one third of the water the older models use (1.6 gallons or just shy of 9 l in the new ones versus 5 gallons or about 23 l in the older ones), so you're already ahead of the game. Got an older toilet? Say, isn't it about time for one of those new low-flow models? I'll bet it is. Just a thought there.

By the way, there has been, since these new low-flow toilets have emerged on the scene, the idea that because they use less water they don't do the job as well and you end up using more water by having to flush repeatedly. While I'm not saying that might not have been true of some earlier models, it would seem as though all concerned have got their act together in that regard, and the new low-flow toilets do work well. No need to flush twice. Or thrice. Or so they say.

There is, of course, the conservative urge to not flush after every use. (All together now: *EEEeeewww*.) That's certainly not everyone's cup of tea (Everyone again: *EEEeeewww.*), but I will say this about that: I seriously doubt that if all you've done is added a thimble full of piddle, you're going to cause the next great cholera outbreak on your block if you don't flush right away. How about this for a reasonable compromise: if you want to give that a go (no pun intended, I assure you), please do us all a favor and add some sort of automatic toilet bowl sanitizer to the tank. That little fellow that zips around in a jaunty yachting cap and motorboat in your toilet tank in the TV commercials seemed nice enough. What ever happened to him?

Let's move on to something a little more pleasant, shall we? How about washing the dishes? These days, at our house, I'm the dishwasher. (And that's Mister Dishwasher to you.) My mother did have one of those big electric automatic ones, and I honestly have no idea what happened to it. It probably went in a yard sale years ago. Fine by me. I never liked it anyway. It was a rolling behemoth and would spray water all over the kitchen when it threw a sort of appliance hissy fit. I do not miss it at all. (Can you tell?)

Since it's just JoAnn and I, we generate very few dishes to wash. (Like, *two*.) And we have had, for years, a long-standing deal: one cooks, the other cleans. These days, JoAnn cooks and I clean. Our dinners at home are great, but seldom elaborate. Cleaning the dishes is no big deal, and I've developed a sort of speed-cleaning system. We have a two-tub sink, and I use one to wash and rinse and the other to dry. The drying side has a stainless steel dish rack nestled down in it.

It works like this: The dirty dishes get stacked on the counter to the left of the sink after dinner. (We're both left-handed, by the way.) With the water running at a low to medium rate, each item gets washed, rinsed, and stacked in the drying rack in the right side tub. With larger items (pots and pans), they get a soak and a serious scrub with the water off, then rinsed before drying. It all takes very little time and seems to use very little water. Much less, I think, than running two big tubs of water (one to wash and one to rinse), then having your dishes sit in both tubs of dirty water. Sort of like the difference between taking a bath and taking a shower. The trick is to work fast and cut the water off when you're wrestling with the big items.

Also, there's an added energy-saving plus to doing the dishes the Uncle Chippie way: I don't use any electricity at all. I throw open the curtains to the kitchen window over the sink and wash those dishes by natural light. I am one energy-saving dishwasher! Plus, my antics seem to amuse the squirrels in the tree outside the window.

Wednesday is laundry day at The Old Haynes Place, and I think JoAnn has a good system in place for saving water while doing that laundry. The washer is out in the garage, allowing her to easily run the washer drain hose out into the yard to water

The greenest white washer in town.

the dry spots with every load. Since we are in the unincorporated part of the county, our home is not hooked up to any municipal sanitary sewer system. We have septic tanks, and it's always a bad idea to let your wash water go into the septic tank. (Yes, our dishwater does, but there's not much of it.) She makes sure she's doing full loads when she does the laundry, which is always a good idea, and the water is drained off through a standard garden hose to various parts of the yard as needed. Doing full loads helps save water, and draining it on the lawn recycles water that would otherwise be lost.

We thought about putting a sprinkler on that hose, and it would probably work, but the lint inherent in the wash water would clog the sprinkler in fairly short order. No need to make washday any more work than it already is. And as it is, JoAnn simply puts the open-ended hose out where needed and the washer does the rest. Water saved, yard watered. A two-for-one deal in resource savings.

Now that we're standing out here in the yard, let's talk about saving water outside. For us, it's almost a total non-event. Aside from draining our laundry wash water in the yard, we don't water the yard at all. As a matter of fact, our home doesn't even have a single outside faucet for that. That sure makes it easy to save water, doesn't it? We used to have an elaborate sprinkler system throughout the yard, and the water for it came from a shallow well and electric pump along the east side of the house. Over time, the sprinkler system gave out, and I finally gave the pump away. I did, however, carefully cap the well, in case we ever needed it again. As a matter of fact, I do have a brand-new cast-iron hand pump set aside for that well, should the need arise. You never know.

It also helps to have drought-tolerant native plants that are used to being wherever you are (no matter where you are). For here, we have a basic landscaping rule that will work just about anywhere: we'll plant it, but after that it's on its own. I might remember to water something I've planted once or twice, but honestly, we don't plant all that much in the way of new stuff, and if it doesn't thrive on neglect, it picked the wrong yard.

One thing I do to help our yard stay green, save water, and use less energy is to mow the grass as high as possible. Taller grass retains more dew every morning, the grass stays greener, and I have to mow less often. These are all good things, especially that last one. I never did see yard work as the whiz-bang way cool hobby you might think it to be, and certainly not the all-consuming passion my neighbors seem to make it. Our yard looks good, it's just not a golf course. I mow the grass and it stays green. What more is there? I don't water, I don't use fertilizer, and if it's green, it's not a weed. It's landscaping.

By the way, while we're out here doing the yard, have I mentioned how much I truly do hate leaf blowers? Yes, I do on occasion use my quiet little shop vac to blow off debris, but by and large, I find that a good, old-fashioned broom works just fine, and often better in tight places like our front porch. The broom uses less power, makes less noise, and you get a decent upper

The leaf blower, mower and edger of the future — sort of

body workout at no extra charge. So do your napping neighbor a favor: use the broom instead of the leaf blower this afternoon. And have you given any thought to a manual edger?

Let's get back to saving water. Have you thought about using the free water that falls on your roof? Rainwater is great if you need additional water for your yard. It can be directed, collected and used as needed, where needed. We make sure ours goes into the yard, and not down the driveway or out in the street. Make good use of that free water!

Having your downspouts empty into rain barrels is a great way to save rain water that might otherwise be wasted, and you can use it when you need it, long after the rain. The truly ambitious will want to know that, yes, you can save that rain water and, with a bit of extra plumbing, use it to fill your toilet tanks. I would not *ever* tell you that you can drink rain water collected in this fashion, as it is a little-known fact that birds do, when you're not looking, poop on your roof. I'm just saying.

If you've got a swimming pool, you know you have an uphill battle when it comes to saving water. You will most definitely want to use a pool cover to control evaporation and water loss when the pool is not in use. Yes, it's a royal pain in the bikini bottom to have to take that cover on and off the pool every time, but it pays off in not having to constantly fill the pool. A pool cover will save you water, but only if you use it.

As for trying to save electricity with a pool, all I can say is keep a close eye on it and make sure you are not overmaintaining the pool. Check the chemical balance in the water frequently to make sure it's safe, but also make sure you aren't doing too much, and using too much power, to keep that pool in good, safe working order.

I've saved the big obvious water saver for last, because I want you to remember it and take it seriously: fix the leaks. That's it. Fix leaks. That's the biggie. Don't let that little drip go on and on and on. It's using water with every drip, and little drips have a funny way of ever so slowly speeding up, virtually unnoticed, until they become quite the steady stream. If you have a faucet that is slowly driving you crazy with that drip, drip, drip, get it fixed! We're here to save water, remember?

One last check of your water system before we move on: turn off all of the water in the house and go out and look at your water meter. Is the little dial thingy spinning? That's a bad sign. That means that, even with all of your water turned off, you're still using water somewhere. This is serious. Go back into the house and make sure everything's off and look again. Check everything. Now look again. Still spinning? You've got a leak. Time to call a plumber. Sorry. I feel your pain.

The Joys of
Solid Waste

O H, THIS IS WHERE we're going to shine. This is where we're going to do some serious good: saving energy, saving resources, and saving a lot of money. I think you're going to really like this chapter. I can hardly wait. I'm excited. Can you tell?

This chapter is going to be all about recycling. And, yes, I know that home recycling has had, in times long past, a certain hippy-dippy earth-shoe smell about it. Relax. This isn't like that at all. We have, over the years, developed an easy, laid-back recycling routine around our house. It's easy to do, it saves us money, and we don't even own a pair of earth shoes.

As I've mentioned, we live in the unincorporated part of the county, outside any and all city limits. That means if we want curbside garbage pickup, we have to pay for it ourselves. For many years (too many years) we did just that, but not anymore. These days, we recycle so much and have so very little left for the garbage man to pick up that we don't bother with curbside pickup at all. By recycling about 95 percent of everything we use and having so very little waste, we save about $500 a year right there. Have I got your attention now? I thought I might.

It began with newspapers. Seems a harmless enough start to the story, doesn't it? We bought a newspaper every day, and often two big ones on Sunday. We still do. All of that news-print adds up to a lot of heavy garbage every week to have to haul down to the curb, and the lovely JoAnn decided it would be easier to simply stack the papers in a bin in the garage and take them to the local recycling center once the bin was full. That's all it took to start a sort of recycling revolution in our home, and now look at us.

These days, we have a system in place to formally recycle about a dozen different things, and to informally recycle many

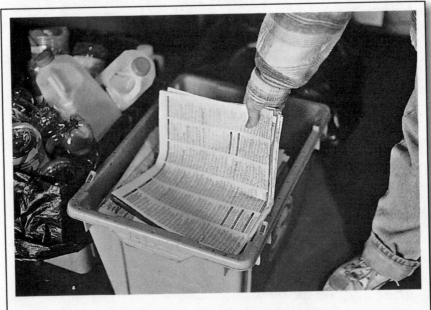

This is how it all started: by recycling newspapers.

more. The difference between the two? I'm glad you asked. "Formal recycling" means we have a dedicated bin for that item, and once that bin is full, the collected item gets delivered to an official recycling center run by the nearest city. The newspapers, for instance, are formally recycled. "Informal recycling" is, as you might imagine, a bit more, well, informal. When I mow the yard, the grass clippings are automatically mulched and left on the yard. That's a great example of informal recycling. Now you know, in case there's a pop quiz on Friday.

How about I simply run down the list of everything we recycle around the house, starting with the things we formally recycle? This will give you a good idea of what you can do around your house, but let me caution you: we did not suddenly start doing all of this serious recycling overnight. Each item was added one at a time, over a period of years. Yes, you can jump right in and do it all at once if you want, but it might go better if you add one item at a time and get used to that. Your call there.

As you know by now, we started our green routine with recycling newspapers. These days, we have a blue recycling bin right outside the door from the dining room to the garage so we can simply open the door and plop the folded papers into the bin in the garage. No muss, no fuss, and very few extra steps. The newspaper bin is our recycle time indicator; that is, when the newspaper bin is full, it's time to go to the recycling center with all of our stuff for formal recycling. With us, that works out to about once every three weeks or so. Maybe once a month if we're not paying attention.

Inside the house, we have a tall wastebasket for mixed paper recycling. This is a huge thing for us, as we end up with a surprising amount of mixed paper. What's mixed paper? Everything

Ready for a trip to the Recycling Center!

but newspapers and corrugated cardboard, it seems. All of our junk mail (and you know how much of that you get every day), old magazines, phone books, scraps of notes I write to myself throughout the day, plain cardboard boxes like cereal and packaged food boxes as well as the empty cardboard tubes from paper towels and toilet paper. The cardboard tubes get scrunched up, and the boxes get folded flat. Any sensitive paperwork with personal information on it goes through a shredder on top of the mixed paper bin before it's recycled. Take no chances. It's worth the electrons to avoid identity theft. Shred the personal stuff. You'll sleep better at night. And don't forget to unplug the shredder.

We don't seem to end up with all that much corrugated cardboard for recycling, but when we do, it gets cut down flat and held for the next trip to the recycling center, where it has its own large bin. I'd be amazed if we ended up with six cardboard boxes a year like that. No idea why we have so little. It's just the way we are.

Right next to the newspaper bin out in the garage is the plastic container bin. This one fills up fast. It seems as though everything we buy these days comes in a plastic container of some sort: milk jugs, peanut butter and jam jars, single-serving-size drink bottles, and almost every non-food item. Everything comes wrapped in plastic, and much of that plastic is recyclable. Look for the little circle of three arrows, the mark of a recyclable item. If there's a number "1" or "2" inside that circle, it's easily recyclable. Check with your local recycling center to make sure you know what plastics they take and what numbers to be looking for. (And what numbers to avoid.) I do look for other uses for many of the plastic items we accumulate and prefer to reuse as opposed to recycle. Nevertheless, I only need so many plastic milk jug mud flaps on my bicycles, and I'm running out of stuff to put in all of those wonderful wide-mouth peanut butter jars. At least they're all recyclable. And by the way, we do rinse out every plastic food container before it goes in the recycling bin. No need to have that stuff sitting in there festering for weeks. Yuck. Keep your recycling clean and sanitary. Please.

You know those cheap plastic shopping bags? The ones you probably shouldn't ever take to begin with? Well, at least if you do take them, they're all recyclable. We keep one hanging in our pantry closet, and when it's full (admittedly, it takes a while), they all go back to the local grocery store for recycling. The store has a big bin for them right out front, so it's easy enough to drop a bag full of bags right in. Done and done, before we even do our shopping. I know the day is fast approaching when we won't bother with those plastic bags at all, ever, but for now, as few as we do get, we do recycle them all.

Do you have any Styrofoam to recycle? We tend to accumulate a few Styrofoam meat trays from the grocery store every month. (Yes, we eat meat. We're, like, cavemen or something. Deal with it.) These are usually small, flat bits of Styrofoam, and they all get put in another plastic bag in the pantry closet after they are washed, just as they all get taken back to the local grocery store where they have yet another big recycling bin just for Styrofoam meat trays and egg cartons. Easy enough.

By the way, I will tell you this: we do our grocery shopping at a Florida-based supermarket chain called Publix. There's a Publix within easy walking distance of our house, and that's what JoAnn does every Thursday: she walks (or rides her big pink tricycle) to the grocery store. If we need something any other day, Publix gets added to the walk we take in the evening. And, yes, we take a canvas bag. (JoAnn sometimes takes a rolling cart on Thursdays.) Publix has been very good about having big bins out front to recycle plastic bags, meat trays and egg cartons. Check the store where you normally shop. If they don't offer recycling bins for those things, you might want to check around and see if any other stores do. I'm not saying you have to shop at those other stores, just know that you can recycle stuff there. We really lucked out with Publix.

Let's talk heavy metal (*Duuuuude*). Metals are all wonderfully recyclable, but there are all different kinds of metals. Around our house, we recycle steel, aluminum, brass and copper. In all honesty, we never do get all that much brass and copper, and when we do, I simply walk over and give it to our next-door neighbor Rudy. He's quite the recycler when it comes to brass and copper, so he's more than welcome to the small amounts we accumulate. Our contribution to his cause will never make him rich, but it does save us from having to figure out what to do with it. That just leaves us with steel and aluminum.

Most of the recyclable steel things we end up with are simply the "tin" cans that food came in. Of course they're not really made of tin any more, but that's what they've been called since they were. In these modern times, our cans get washed out, rinsed and dried after use, their lids dropped down inside, and the can itself goes into a smaller bin in the garage, just the other side of the big plastic containers bin. I also tend to generate a small amount of steel in the form of broken bike parts, and these are also thrown in the bin if I can't find another use for them around the garage.

Ah, aluminum! We generate surprisingly little aluminum, but it's all so recyclable. Since neither of us drinks a lot of soda or anything stronger that might come in a can, most of our recycled aluminum comes from the aluminum foil we use in cooking. Again, like the empty food cans, the used foil is washed, rinsed and dried before it gets folded up and pitched into the appropriate bin in the garage. And, yes, broken alloy bike parts suffer the same fate, minus the wash and rinse.

I know it sounds kind of prissy to wash and rinse some of the stuff we recycle, but anything that had food or drink in it or on it has the potential to become a sort of lower life form in the recycle bin before it gets carted off to the center several weeks later. This is, after all, warm and humid Florida. Things tend to grow here, often quite well. We rinse out all containers and wash off anything that had contact with food. Better safe than having to hire a haz-mat team to decontaminate the garage.

Obviously, that wash and rinse routine goes for glass as well. Again, we're talking mostly about food containers here, so, yes, they all get washed and rinsed before they go into their own special bin in the back of the garage, where they won't get broken. Any metal lids to those glass containers get put in the metal bin, of course.

The funny thing is, we can do almost all of our formal recycling at one center up in Clearwater. Everything but glass. The glass has to go to Largo, the next town south. No idea why Clearwater doesn't handle glass and Largo does, but it's a small price to pay to recycle everything that we do recycle. And we accumulate very little glass. JoAnn might have to make maybe two glass runs a year. Maybe. That's why we make sure it's all clean before it goes in the bin. That glass may sit there for a while. Oh, and I hesitate to use glass containers in the garage. They don't bounce all that well off of a concrete floor. Voice of experience there.

The other major formal recycling thing we do is we recycle our motor oil. I change my own oil in our truck, the motorcycle, the motor scooter and the lawn mower. The gas chainsaw is set up with no oil to change, so we get a pass there. This is so easy: the used oil simply goes back to the store where we bought the new oil. Almost all auto parts stores around here offer oil recycling at no charge. Just take the used stuff back and dump it in their big drum. (Ask first if they offer this service!) A total piece of cake. I also make sure I drain the oil filter and add that oil to the mix, and I use a reusable container to store and deliver the used oil back to the store. Every little bit helps.

That's about it for the formal stuff. On the informal side of the equation, we still do a lot of recycling. Out in the yard, I recycle the lawn clippings and the fallen tree limbs, each in their own way. I have, for years, simply cut the grass and let the clippings fall where they may, right there in the yard. And that works, but now I make it even better: I mulch. I got all ambitious a while back and built a steel mulching plate to go over our mower's cut grass exhaust vent. (Actually, it's bolted to the inside of the mowing deck.) Now whatever is cut is cut into much finer pieces and drops right there under the mower and into the lawn. No more rows of cut grass clumps, browning in the sun, and the mower is much quieter and cleaner to operate. It no longer flings great clouds of dust and dirt and debris. I like that. And I guarantee you, the next time I have to buy a new lawn mower, it will be designed and built as a mulching mower right from the start. Short of hiring a herd of goats, it's the only way to go.

I mentioned earlier how many trees we have in our yard, and with all of those trees comes a steady supply of fallen tree limbs. Lucky us. This can get especially crazy during our summer storm season (also known around here as Hurricane Season, by the way), but a big wind can come through here any time and offer up a fine collection of dead wood all over the yard. How nice. Ah, well, picking it all up is good exercise, right? I keep a large bin in the garage for tree limbs and yard debris, and when it's full, I build up a little fire in the fireplace and spend the evening reading a book and feeding the fire.

Those tree limbs don't go alone, by the way. Since we recycle our newspapers, and not burn them, the question did arise: what do we do for kindling to start these tree limb fires? The answer: "combustibles." We informally recycle our combustibles.

In almost every room of the house, in every room that would have a trash can, there are two trash cans, side by side. One is for garbage that can't be recycled or burned. The other is for combustibles. So what goes in the combustibles can? Paper towels, paper napkins and tissues go in that can, to be used to start the fires in the fireplace. Paper towels I've used in the garage, working on bikes, go in their own special can in the garage, also to be added to the fire. Anything that can't be recycled but can be burned goes into the nearest combustibles container. That gives us plenty of kindling for the tree limb fires. Even cotton swabs, if they have wrapped paper stems, go in with the other combustibles. Burn, baby, burn.

Having two bins makes it all work.

All of this becomes a wonderful, cozy reading fire about once a month, and after several months of small, cozy reading fires, the ash from the fireplace gets shoveled into a steel pail and spread out on the lawn. It's the big circle of life if you're a dead tree branch in our yard. Or a used paper napkin.

Getting our home set up for all of this recycling took time. It was all done over months and years, and, yes, there were more than a few missteps along the way. Our biggest misstep came when we seriously overestimated how much garbage we would have to throw away. Seriously.

At one point, I had called our County Solid Waste Department and asked what it would cost to simply haul our garbage to the landfill on our own. We do, after all, have a truck. The answer was "$10 a truckload," which seemed more than reasonable, considering how much garbage our truck would hold and what we were paying for curbside garbage pickup at the time. Armed with that information, I proceeded to set up our garage to store the garbage in large sealed cans until we had enough to make the trip to the landfill worthwhile. I wanted to get my ten dollars' worth. I built a long, tall shelf to hold all of our recycle bins over a series of three or four large (55-gallon or 210-liter) garbage cans. The plan was to keep the garbage in sealed yard bags in the sealed cans, then load the bags onto the truck when it was time to go. The plan, like so many of my plans, seemed like a good idea at the time. My cunning plan went all pear-shaped after JoAnn gently reminded me that we could also burn our tree limbs and yard waste in the fireplace instead of hauling it all to the landfill, and that doing so would save us even more time, energy and certainly money. By adding that "combustibles" category to our informal recycling system, we seriously streamlined our green routine. Now all I had to do was to figure what to do with those brand-new big garbage cans we didn't need at all.

The garbage cans were given willingly to my wonderful mother-in-law, who has a large wooded yard in Largo. She could certainly make good use of them. (The city picks up her yard debris.) The shelf I had built for the recycling bins was disassembled, the wood reused, and the bins themselves now reside on the garage floor, under a line of bicycles hanging from hooks from a much higher shelf. *Whew*. We never did make the first run to the landfill, saving us the $10 fee and the gas to get there and back again. Money and energy saved all around, even if we did spin our wheels there for a bit.

These days, all of our recycle bins except the one for the newspapers are lined with heavy (reusable!) plastic yard bags. This allows JoAnn to simply gather up the bags of recyclable materials and throw them in the back of the truck when it's time to go. This also keeps the bins clean. The newspapers are far too heavy for that trick, so for them, the whole bin goes for a ride in the cab, to keep them from all blowing away as she drives down the road. I think we've got a pretty good system going these days, but we're always looking for ways to make it better.

Of course, we also have all of those double trash cans around the house for combustibles and non-combustibles, but we've gotten so used to using them, we don't notice them at all. It doesn't seem at all odd to have two cans, side by side, where most people have but one. It's our green routine, and just part of living small. And it's easy.

Let me shift green gears here for a minute and tell you that a lot of people are surprised to find out that we don't have a big compost heap or rotating compost bin in the back yard. And we really don't. There's no need. At one point some time ago, we both went over to the County Cooperative Extension Service and took a free class on composting that came with a free compost bin. You sure can't beat an offer like that, unless you find out that you don't need it at all. And that's what we found out.

After sitting through the class and taking the tour of the grounds, we found that composting requires a whole lot more material to work with than we would ever generate. A cubic yard's worth, in fact, to generate the heat needed to break down the debris and waste. That's a lot of garbage. It would have taken us *years* to have that much stuff to compost. It was a great idea for a large family with a lot of food waste, but for just the two of us, it wasn't going to work. I won't say I was terribly disappointed, but it was nice to know that we're doing so well with our green routine that we don't even generate enough garbage to make traditional composting work for us. Still, we do compost. Sort of.

We, and by "we" I mean JoAnn, are very careful about buying food with an eye toward not buying food waste. This means boneless (and preferably "fatless") cuts of meat and veggies that don't generate a lot of waste. We try to not end up with a lot of food waste, as we rely on in-ground composting to get rid of what we don't eat. For us, that means the occasional banana peel and maybe some egg shells once in a great while. What little kitchen waste we have is dropped into yet another (very small) sealed container, and after dinner, after the dishes are all done and dried and put away, one of us heads out to the back yard and buries the waste. And *that*, ladies and gentlemen, is in-ground composting: you simply bury it in the

Buried treasure, matey? Nah, just a bit of composting.

back yard. And let me tell you: this is working out much better than expected.

We have one small shovel that we use to bury the banana peels, and I've been burying them in the area out back where this house used to have a water softener. Over the years, before it was removed, the water softener leached (leaked) salt into the ground. Now I'm trying to offset that by adding more organic material where the softener used to be. Do keep in mind that this is Florida, where we don't really have any dirt as such. All we have is sand, and lots of it. It's going to take a lot of old banana peels to turn that salt-damaged sand into real dirt. I can start to see a difference, but we're going to need a lot more bananas. It's a good thing I like bananas.

So, with all of the recycling we do, both formal and informal, the combustibles and the fireplace and in-ground composting, how much do we really have left to throw away? And what could possibly be *left* to throw away? Admittedly, not very much.

In the bathroom, we pitch the used toothpaste tubes and worn-out disposable razor blades, along with empty shaving cream cans that seem to last forever. (The plastic deodorant thingies are recyclable, by the way.) In the kitchen, certain food packaging is simply not recyclable, and I see the same thing out in the garage. There is some stuff that you simply have to throw away. Most of these things are of mixed content: they contain both metal and plastic not easily separated. Our truck's air filter, for instance, is made of paper, plastic *and* metal. What do you do? I throw them away. I'm not going to sit there and pick them apart. Not yet, anyway. Maybe after I'm retired.

Overall, we throw away so very little that we can't recycle that, at the end of a month's time, when it's time to go to the recycle center, we have but a small kitchen bag full of trash that can't be recycled. The recycle centers all offer regular trash bins for non-recyclables, and that's where it goes. (What little there is.)

We are, understandably, very careful about what we bring home in the first place. Judicious acquisition is the key to success! We look at everything before we buy it with an eye to how we're going to get rid of it when the time comes. Do we really need it? Is it recyclable? If not, what happens when it breaks, wears out, or is used up? How are we going to dump this thing? We make periodic clothing donations to the local thrift stores, and once in a blue moon we have a monster yard sale. Still, the best thing is to limit how much you bring in. No garbage in, no garbage out. And recycle the rest.

8

Surviving with Smaller Transportation

OH, I COULD WRITE a whole book about this one. No, wait, I did. We'll talk more about *The Practical Cyclist* a bit later. For now, we need to talk about living small when you're not at home. Maybe we should call this "traveling green." No one should live their life in just one spot, unmoving. Don't sit at home. You need to get out and see the world. The world needs to see you. Even if all you do is walk around the block, get out there and see that block! You just have to be a little green about it, that's all.

In these times of higher energy costs, transportation is the one place where we see a big chance to go small. A surprisingly high percentage of our daily travel is really quite discretionary. That is, we probably don't really have to go at all. Yes, when you've got to go, you've got to go, but — do you really? Is this trip really necessary? Maybe now would be a good time to take serious stock of where you go and how you get there.

The first rule of traveling green: never, ever *drive* to the Earth Day celebration. I'm just saying. JoAnn and I recently rode our bicycles to the local annual Living Green Expo, and I have to tell you: the parking lot was full — of cars. We were not the only people to pedal there, but cars outnumbered bicycles by about one hundred to one, at least. It was funny, and yet it was no laughing matter. At least *we* didn't have to worry about finding a parking space. We chained our bikes to the railing by the front door and had a wonderful time. Carpe velo. (Seize the bike.)

Traveling green is all about living in a smaller monkeysphere. "Monkeysphere" is a fun word that was coined to describe the amount of social/group information one monkey can accept and process. Smarter monkeys are able to accept a wider circle of other monkeys, a larger monkeysphere, but every monkey has his (or her) limit. I use the word to describe the territory any one person can easily cover and still be green. For the average monkey, er, person, that would be a radius of about three miles (or five kilometers) from home. Three miles is a good average for your personal monkeysphere. You can, if you're in fair shape, easily walk three miles in one hour. With a bicycle, you can ride three miles in about fifteen or twenty minutes, no problem. Ten minutes if you really want to, but let's not push it. Relax and allow half an hour.

Traveling green, and living in that smaller monkeysphere, means traveling less. And traveling less is good when your goal is to live small, right? It's not about *doing* less. It's about doing what you do, but using less (and traveling less) to do it. It's about using less energy and fewer resources, especially those pesky non-renewable resources we hear so much about these days. It's about using less expensive gasoline and fuel, and you know how much we're hearing about *that* these days. Traveling green can help.

Of course I'm going to tell you some things you've probably heard before. They do bear repeating. Combine your trips. That helps a lot. Really plan where you're going to go before you just set out with no clear goal in mind. We've all done that, and we all need to not do that any more. Our days of mindless driving are so over. Know where you need to go and try to group your destinations close together. This works no matter how you plan to get there: on foot, by bike, or in your car. By taking a few minutes to plan your trip and combining your destinations, you can save a lot of time, money and energy with every trip. And yet, you still get to go. Just go green.

Obviously, you can save even more if you don't go at all. Sometimes staying home is the best choice, but, yes, I get as stir-crazy as the next monkey. Sometimes I just want to get out of my tree, er, house! Plan your trips, choose your route, then choose your mode of transport wisely. You can get there, you just need to get there using less.

As I mentioned earlier, JoAnn and I have several gasoline-powered modes of transportation in addition to all of our bi-cycles and tricycles. We have a full-size pickup truck with a full-size gas engine. (Well, a V6, anyway.) We also have a 500cc motorcycle and a 200cc motor scooter. The scooter has a sidecar on it, making it very practical for around-town jaunts. We try to match the machine to the trip and not take anything larger than we need for where we're going. Close to home, we walk or ride bikes. Across town? Bicycles or the scooter. To the far side of the county? It's the motorcycle or truck. Out of the county in the rainy season? Definitely the truck.

The idea here is to be able to get by with the smallest form of transportation possible to meet your needs and still let you travel safe. You have to balance being green with being practical. There's also only so much room in anyone's garage, and our garage is full right now. With all of those bicycles, there's no room for another car. Not even an electric one. When it comes to traveling green, it's time for you to sit down and figure out where it is you want to go, and how best to get there.

It seems as though, throughout North America, everyone needs a car. Unless you live in the center of a very large city with great mass transit, you're going to need some sort of motorized machine to get you where you need to go. If you don't, consider yourself very lucky indeed. Me? I live in suburbia. It's suburbia

sometimes better mileage is fun!

as far as the eye can see. Yes, I can walk or ride my bicycle to a great many of my normal destinations, but there are times when that's not enough, and mass transit isn't going to cut it. There are simply times when I have to drive. In the long run, in the years ahead, I know that our big truck will be replaced by something smaller. Probably something *much* smaller. As is so often the case with going green and living small, downsizing your transportation becomes a sort of limbo: how low (how small) can you go? Let's find out!

As I write this in May of 2008, we're just now starting to see true microcars being offered for sale in America. The Mercedes Smart is the new "in" car but still has a very long waiting list. I do, however, see them on the road, and that's a good sign. The Smart is a cool little car. The French/Canadian ZENN (Zero Emission, No Noise) electric car is starting to show up around here as well, and it looks great. We'll see if anyone buys one. (I have yet to see one in private hands or out on the road.) There are a handful of three-wheel cars with small motor-scooter engines being offered here, but I only see these rented by tourists, for now. We're going to need more choices to broaden our micocar market, and we need them right now.

When it comes to choices, I know many people think their only choices for traveling green are gas or electric. In truth, it's gas, electric or diesel, but let's talk about the electric vehicle option first. Many people think electric vehicles are pollution free and use no non-renewable resources. That's not entirely true. All vehicles, even shoes and bicycles, have already used an amazing amount of resources and energy just in their manufacture. Electric cars are no different, and all of those batteries are far more toxic than even my smelly sneakers. In operation, electric vehicles are not exactly pollution-free. They just don't carry their tail pipe with them. Electric vehicles simply transfer the point of pollution to the power plant that generated the electricity that charged the batteries. You might say that they are *external* combustion engines. They still pollute, you just don't see it. Unless you drive by the power plant.

Yes, if you charge up your electric vehicle with a wind turbine generator or a photovoltaic solar panel, then there's no pollution in operation. (Only in manufacture.) So, how many of you plan to do just that? Not many hands going up out there, but that's OK. There are (thankfully) other green solutions.

One company in California offers a three-wheel electric car with a huge solar panel over the entire roof. I like that! Do the roof-mounted solar panels work well enough to keep the car charged as you use it? Probably not, but it sure is a big step in the right direction. Go team!

So the idea here is to end up with the smallest car or truck possible that still meets your needs. Additionally, it's probably also a very good idea to try to eliminate the need for two vehicles. (Yes, I know: I have three. So sue me.) What I mean is, if you have a big truck and a small car, could you maybe get by with a single smaller truck? Assuming, of course, that you really need that truck. We really use our truck as a truck, but, yes, when the time comes, I suspect our next one will be smaller.

The first thing you need to be aware of when you go shopping for that smaller vehicle (car or truck) is that it's not about the number of cylinders, but the overall engine displacement. No, you probably don't want a V8 in your next machine, but you can end up with a six-cylinder engine that has a larger overall displacement than an eight-cylinder one, and that's a step in the wrong direction. What's the difference between cylinders and displacement? Sit down. Get comfy. I'll explain.

When you see "V8" or "V6" on any machine, that means the engine has six or eight pistons moving within the cylinders inside that engine to generate the power by compressing the fuel/air mixture that's fed into them. That tells you virtually nothing about the overall size of the engine. Moto-Guzzi, the Italian motorcycle manufacturer, made a V8 motorcycle engine back in the 1950s that only displaced 500cc. The engine was a miniature work of art. Cadillac, on the other hand, offered an 8200cc leviathan of a V8 in the early 1970s. It was not a work of art, but it was a piece of work. "Beast" didn't begin to describe it. That Caddy probably got 8 miles to the gallon (about 3½ km/l) on a good day. Downhill, with a tail wind and the engine off. If you were lucky.

The moral of the story here is to not focus so much on the number of cylinders you're being offered. It's all about the displacement of those cylinders or, more accurately, the amount of space displaced by the movement of the pistons within the cylinders as the engine runs. One piston moves up and down in every cylinder in any engine. (And we'll not be confusing the issue with the Wankel rotary engine, now, will we?) The amount of space each piston moves through is the displacement of that piston. Multiply that piston displacement by the number of cylinders in the engine, and you have the engine's total displacement. The engine's total displacement is a far truer gauge of the engine's size and potential thirst for fuel. And what you're looking for here is the smallest possible displacement that will still get the job done. The number of cylinders hardly matters at all. Now you know. Make good choices.

Next question: gas or diesel? Deal? Or no deal? (Sorry. Couldn't resist.) If you're anywhere near average in North America, you've been around gasoline engines all your life. Diesel-powered private vehicles are a little more exotic and too often have that truck-stop cache attached to them. I owned a small diesel car some thirty years ago, and, yes, back then, it did smell like a truck stop, good buddy.

The latest diesels do not smell so much like that truck stop you wouldn't pull into on a dare, no matter how bad you needed that restroom. Cleaner diesel fuel and far better technology in private diesel-powered vehicles have made them far more socially acceptable these days. They are, I'm told, all the rage in Europe. We are already seeing this new diesel technology in North America, and odds are you see diesel cars every day and don't realize that they are what they are. I say all of this to make a small point: don't rule out a diesel for your next small car. It might be the right choice. You never know.

Car, truck or SUV? Sedan, station wagon or convertible? Regular or extra crispy? As with everything else in life, we all have choices to make. Maybe too many choices, when it comes to what we drive. It's too easy to drive too much. So how much do you really need? How *little* do you really need?

It's just JoAnn and I, so we can get by with a two-seater. But we also have bicycles and tricycles and stuff, and we sometimes need to haul large things as well. For us, the pickup truck makes sense. Yes, we could get by with a smaller pickup truck, but this was the one we saw on the used car lot at the dealership, and it spoke to us.

We have friends with children, who need a machine to move all of them at once, together with everything that goes along with having children. And you know how that goes: families always have stuff. For them, they need a four-seater with a good amount of weather-proof, lockable cargo space. They could not get by with our open-bed pickup truck, just as we don't need anything as large as what they drive. We all have different needs. How many people in your family? How much stuff do you have to bring along? How far do you want to go? And how far do you *have* to go? Somewhere in there is your answer.

Look at what might fit your needs, then ask about engine displacement. Are there engine options? Can you get that thing with a smaller engine? Some cars and trucks have engine options, but many don't. If you can get the machine you want with the smallest engine available, that's a step in the right direction, but how small is small?

Since most engine displacements today are measured in cubic centimeters or liters (1 liter = 1000cc), let's stick with that for comparison, shall we? Our truck has a 4.3-liter (4300cc) V6. That, to me, is huge, and certainly more power than we need. I think my last truck had half of that. My next truck most certainly will. If you can find a car or truck with an engine with less than 2 liters (2000cc) displacement, that would be a great start toward living small and traveling green. My old '66 VW had a 1300cc engine, and it got me everywhere I needed to go. Was I in less of a hurry back then? Nope. You really don't need the biggest engine you can find. You never did. Sometimes you have to work at living small, but that effort pays off every time you stop at the gas station. Especially these days. Buy small, live small, travel green.

One option I want to take off the table right now is the gas-powered golf cart. I know it's cute, and it looks like it's fun to drive down the road without the golf clubs rattling around off the back, but let me tell you: they get lousy gas mileage. Seriously lousy gas mileage. Voice of experience here.

Some time ago, I had the chance to go out and do all new field research for a local recreational trail guidebook. Knowing the length of the trail (some 35 miles or 55 km at the time), the rangers patrolling it offered me the use of a gas-powered golf cart and a uniformed ranger to drive me down to the southern end of the trail and back, so I could make quick work of my research on that end of the trail. I took them up on their kind offer and met the ranger and his golf cart at their main office near the middle of the trail. He topped off the gas tank that morning, and off we went.

Yes, it was fun to zip down the trail all noise and fumes and speed. We made good time and covered a lot of ground, far more than I would have had I elected to do that same distance on my bicycle, and it was certainly faster than doing it on foot. Judging by the maps I had brought along, we did a 25-mile (or 40-kilometer) round-trip that day with the golf cart, about twice what I could have covered without it. Gee, golf carts are great! Or maybe not.

The next day, before we set off for the next section of the trail, the ranger topped off the little gas tank in that golf cart, just as he had done the day before. It took two gallons. It took a moment for that to sink in: two gallons. We only went 25 miles (40 km). That's 12½ miles to the gallon (5¼ km/l). That's seriously lousy gas mileage. Because golf carts don't come with odometers, you never know how far you've gone. We knew how far we'd gone. We had the maps. I *did* the maps. We had the mileage. It was a real eye opener. I had no idea. Now we both do. Consider yourself fairly warned and avoid gas-powered golf carts.

Yes, electric golf carts might be a better deal, if all you're doing is zipping around in your close neighborhood, no more than, say, a level mile (or two kilometers) from home. That might work, but I say *might*. A lot depends on the roads and traffic in your neighborhood, and whether or not it's even legal to run a golf cart on the streets where you live. You might want to check that out first. Generally speaking, a bicycle or tricycle would be a far better choice for as little as any golf cart, gas or electric, can really do for you.

With ever-higher gas prices these days, I'm seeing more and more very small motor scooters on our roads down here in Florida. These are colorful little 49cc two-stroke machines, all of them (it would seem) from way over on the west side of the Pacific Ocean. Cheap to buy, cheap to run, and virtually disposable when they break down, these small scooters are helping many people use less gas and still get around. Would this work for you?

It might. I wouldn't want to go more than about five miles from home on one, but that's just me. You'd have to be able to take the smaller, slower roads, as they seems to top out at about 25 to 30 mph (40 to 50 km/h). It also helps that we have no long, steep hills around here. These things don't have a lot of reserve power. Still, it beats driving your big car, and if this might work for you, why not? They sure look like fun!

I will say this about these small motor scooters: if you're going to buy one, buy a good one. Buy a name brand that you recognize. At least three of the four major Japanese motorcycle manufacturers also make scooters. We also see some great European motorcycle makers represented here with scooters as well. Buy a name. Yes, you can get the off-brand machine for considerably less, but know that you are buying an orphan with very little (if any) dealer support and virtually no supply line for parts. And you will, eventually, need parts. I've seen too many cheap scooters thrown away for the lack of a $5 part they couldn't get. If you're going to get one, get a good one. And make sure you can get the parts.

When it comes to motor scooters, and especially to motor-cycles, it's very easy to buy more bike than you need. If a 50cc scooter will get you across town (and it usually will), then a 250cc motor scooter should get you just about anywhere you need to go, within reason. We had a 250cc Japanese motor scooter for years and took it everywhere, even up on the Interstate at Inter-state speeds. Two up. It flew. It did everything we needed, and it got 50 miles to the gallon (21 km/l). We wore it out. I wouldn't mind another.

We also have a 500cc motorcycle, and let me tell you: it will get you where you need to go *right now*. For practical speed and power, I don't know why you'd need anything larger. We sure don't. If you go shopping for a scooter or motorcycle, don't let anyone tell you that you need a big, fast, powerful (expensive) machine to get around. You can scare yourself silly with cheap 50cc scooters. In town, they go fast enough. If you want to get out on the highway and get your motor running, look at a 250cc scooter or cycle. Anything above that is gravy. Our 500cc is all that and more. Rock and roll.

If you opt for the smallest thing you can find, and they do make things smaller than the 50ccs, please make sure what you're buying is actually street legal. A lot of the tiny stuff is not. We see a lot of "go-peds" around here. These are little more that two-wheeled skateboards with a 32cc motor. No seat, no lights, and not in any way, shape or form street legal. They aren't legal on the road, they aren't legal on the sidewalk, and they sure aren't legal on any recreational trail. They are legal *nowhere*, and yet here they are. How do they get away with it? The police have better things to do, I guess.

To make sure your ride is legal, you ask the police, not the person who's selling it to you. I'll be real polite here and say that the seller may not have accurate, up-to-date information on that subject. Or they could just lie to sell you the illegal machine. Life's funny that way, and no laughing matter if you get caught. Or hit.

First order of business: know where you need to go, then make sure you look at all of your options for getting there safely, efficiently and legally. Define your travel needs before you rush out and buy that cool shiny scooter from far-off Frapsnotistan just because it was on sale, this week only, last one available, all sales are final. Do pass on that one.

By the way, did you know that Harley-Davidson used to make a motor scooter? It was called the Topper, featured a 175cc engine, and came with a cool two-tone paint job and a pull start like a lawn mower. That's one hog I'd be happy to make room for in my garage. Maybe if we all ask real nice, they'll make it again. What do you think?

You might have one other motorized option here when it comes to living small and traveling green: mass transit. Just get on the bus, Gus. Do we need to discuss much? I think maybe we do. In many towns around North America, the only mass transit available (if there's any available at all) is the municipal bus system. Bus systems range from dreadful to delightful, and you never know what you're going to get. The funny thing is,

I've heard our own local bus system here described as both. I guess it's all about your expectations and personal adaptability. If you're going to ride the bus, you have to be *ready* to ride the bus, and that means armed with enough information to make it work for you, no matter how it works.

Start with acquiring a general bus system route map for your area, one that shows where every bus route goes. Is there a bus route near you? Have you seen the bus stop signs near your house? That's where you're going to start (and hopefully end up). That's where you get on the bus. Now: how much is it? Know the fares before you board, and you'll probably want to

You can take the bus and relax.

have the exact change ready for your fare. (Most bus drivers do not make change. That's not what they're there for.) Can you get a daily pass? That is, can you pay one flat fee and ride the bus as much as you want, all day? Around here, you can get daily, weekly and monthly passes, with discounts offered to both students and seniors. Riding the bus can be downright cheap around here, and yet few people do it. More people should.

The key to making the bus system work for you is to carefully study the route map to understand how the system works. Does the bus go where you want to go? Can it get you to work on time? How close can it get you to work? Can it get you to shopping or to school or to the movies? And, equally importantly, can it get you back home again? Study the maps and the timetables carefully. It can be a long walk (or an expensive cab ride) back home if you get it wrong or it doesn't work.

If you're going to ride the bus, I strongly recommend that you test ride it first. That means setting aside one day (one whole day) to get out there and explore the bus system just to see how it works, where the buses go, and how long it takes to get to your destination. Set yourself a reasonable goal for a destination, and see if you can make the bus system work to get you there and back again. Do keep in mind that the bus system's weekend schedule may be quite different from its regular weekday schedule, so if you're doing this to eventually ride to work and back, you might want to try this test on a regular work day. (Take the day off, obviously.) Dress for comfort, and make sure you wear good shoes for both standing and walking. You might be out on the road for a while, and there's no need to swap dwarfs while you're out there. (Leave Happy, return Grumpy, and, yeah, feel a little Dopey about half way through.)

It pays to ask questions before you go. Most bus systems have special helpline phone numbers and extensive web sites to help their riders (especially their new ones) get around and make the most of what they offer. Riding the bus isn't free, and it does take more time to ride the bus than if you simply drove yourself there in the first place, but you can save energy, resources and money in the long run if the system works in your favor.

One thing that really works in your favor when it comes to riding the bus is the Bikes on Buses program, if your local bus system has such a program. Around here, every bus on every route has a spiffy three-bike bike rack that folds down at the front of the bus to hold your bike if you want to ride that bus. You can bring your bike along for the ride, and it doesn't cost any more than a regular fare. Is that a great deal or what?

When this Bikes on Buses program first began around here, you had to spend $2 for a special permit card (a one-time purchase, good forever) that told the bus driver that you had seen the video and taken the short class that showed you how to work the bike rack on the front of the bus. I passed that class with flying colors. Top of my class (of one). After a few years, our local bus system dropped the whole permitting process thing, and now you just show up at the bus stop with your bicycle and figure it all out when the bus shows up. It's not that hard. Oh, and by the way: the racks on the front of the buses are not meant for tandem bicycles or tricycles. You need to know that, just in case you get any bright ideas beforehand. Like I did.

Ah, but what do you do if you brought your regular, normal bike to the bus stop, and the bus pulls up with a full rack of bikes? *Uh-oh.* Now what? Well, you could wait for the next bus, but if it's a popular route for cyclists, that next bus's bike rack might be full as well. You could ride your bike to where you wanted to go, but if you were going to take the bus, you probably had a good reason to not ride your bike. So what do you do? What do you do? Here's a happy answer (again with that dwarf thing): have you given any thought to owning a folding bike? Now might be a good time to give yourself that thought.

I'm going to bore you to tears here in a minute with far more than you every wanted to know about bicycles, but for now, I need to tell you that many bus systems allow you to bring a folded bicycle right on the bus with you, just as you would a folded baby carriage, for instance. The bike should be folded before the bus gets to your stop, and the folded bike needs to be kept out of the main aisle after you board and find a seat, but it can be done, and it shouldn't cost you any more than your regular fare. I am, despite my lack of height, a huge fan of folding bikes. (Can you tell?) This is just another reason to own one. If you do plan to try this clever option for multi-modal travel, please do call your local bus system ahead of time and find out for sure if they allow this sort of cleverness. And if they don't, ask why not.

While that pretty much sums up our options when it comes to combining living small, traveling green, and using motorized transport, we have, in the timeless (if somewhat mutated) words of Karen C., only just begun to explore our green options in getting around. When it comes to serious options for low-impact travel, there are, honestly, only three alternatives to using oil: walk, ride a bike, or stay home. We're going to assume, for the sake of both argument and this book, that you are not going to stay home. Good for you. You go, (fill in gender-related reference of your choice here). Now that just leaves two options, but they're both good ones: either you walk or you ride your bicycle. There are some fine arguments for both.

When it comes to walking or riding a bicycle, it's all about options that don't involve driving your car. Not driving your car, despite TV commercials to the contrary, is good. Very good, in fact. If you choose to walk or ride a bicycle to get around, you are saving yourself money, keeping yourself healthy, using fewer non-renewable resources, and making the world a better place. You should get a medal. Just using your car a little less makes a big difference in your impact on the world around you. This is what living small and being green is all about, and here's the deep, dark secret: it's also the most fun. No joke. Let's look at walking first. It's really easy. You can do it already, I'll bet.

I'm a great one for making lists. Sometimes I have lists of lists, but you don't need to know that. That's just weird. What you want to do to line up your walking options is to start a list of every business and potential destination within one mile of your house. (And no, please don't rush right out and drive a mile in every direction. Just guess.) You want to know what's really out there, you want to know exactly where they are, what their hours are, and it wouldn't hurt to have their phone number handy, just in case. Nothing more annoying than walking to some business a mile away that's closed because you didn't call first and their hours changed. (Well, maybe there are some things more annoying than that, but it's still no fun.) I just rode my bicycle to a bike shop the other day that was unexpectedly closed on Wednesdays. (And I say "unexpectedly" because I never bothered to read the hours clearly posted on their front door. Duh.) Who knew? Not me, obviously. Ah, well, it was a nice ride. *Still...*

Generally speaking, just about anyone can walk a mile or two comfortably. Yes, you can. You're not going to break any speed records, but you can get there and back in good time. What's "good time"? You should be able to cover a mile on foot in about twenty minutes. That's three miles an hour. You can do it. I do it all the time, and look at me. The trick is to start out slow and close to home with shorter walks, and work your way out from there. You don't have to go any faster, just a little further. You'll be stepping off a mile or two in no time, and feeling very good about it. Try to not look so smug.

Maybe start with this: what's the closest place you could possibly walk to for dinner? Is there any place within a mile of your house? There you go. Walk to dinner, then walk home again. Two miles round trip, tops. Just promise me this: if you do this, treat yourself to dessert. You earned it. Cheers.

So why in the world would anyone want to walk anywhere? Are there really any joys to be had in walking? I think so. Even without all the advantages of being green, saving the planet, and saving yourself all of that money, walking really gets you in shape. Walking is, by far, the best way to really and truly see the world you live in. It gives

Backpack and umbrella — ready to walk

you time to appreciate the world around you, the town you're a part of, and the planet you share with 6.6 billion other people. And I'll bet you don't know half of them, do you? See? You need to get out and walk more. Don't be such a wallflower.

On foot you get to see more, hear more, interact more, and, yes, smell more than you would if you moved through life and across the planet's surface any other way. Even, I have to say, on a bicycle. On foot, you are a complete and integral part of your neighborhood and the world around you. You *are* the neighborhood. It's really cool. JoAnn and I do a tremendous amount of walking these days, and it has given us an intimate knowledge of our small corner of the globe. We see things on foot we would never see any other way. Things that no one else could possibly see. Even the bicycle can be too fast to catch the small details of such a finite place. The devil may be in the details, but so are the fascination, beauty and humor. You don't get that stuff driving in a car. You really need to go for a walk.

After telling you to walk a mile, you need to know that JoAnn and I sometimes walk five miles, round trip, when we go out to dinner. A normal evening's walk for us (after dinner) is four miles, but we're used to it. We sure didn't start out pacing major mileage like that. We started out small with short walks. Very short walks. Like, just around the block. The key to success in walking is to work your way up to those miles gradually, over weeks and months.

Still, despite our mileage, we haven't really boosted our pace. We meander along at a fairly steady three miles an hour (five kilometers an hour for you metric types), and our pace never really varies all that much. We do stop to talk to our neighbors and pet the dogs. We are not in a hurry, nor should you be. If you can't

walk and talk, you're walking too fast. The casual pace will get
you there in better shape. Life is not a race.

So how much can you do on foot? That depends. How close
do you live to the things that you need, and are you at least
a little bit adventurous? I have yet to haul a full sheet of ply-
wood home from the hardware store on foot, but I'll tell you
this: I could (and I would) if I had to. For now, I try to limit my
struggles on foot and only carry a few lighter items, usually in a
belt pack, shoulder bag, or backpack. JoAnn, on foot, routinely
brings home a week's worth of groceries in a rolling cart, although she did admit she used her big pink tricycle last week.
(Cool!) I try to not end up carrying stuff home in a bag held by
hand. It invariably bangs against my knees, and I don't care for

The answer to "Paper or plastic?" is "Neither!"

that at all. I find no virtue in pain. Go for, at the very least, some sort of messenger type bag with a shoulder strap. I prefer a backpack to center the load, but that's just me. Anything beats dragging those cheap plastic shopping bags for blocks that cut into your hands and wrists and stretch to the breaking point three blocks from home. No one wants that. Do you?

We have, around our humble home, a huge variety of things to carry things. From small canvas shopping bags to a wide range of belt packs and backpacks from size small to size expedition — we can carry things. Lots of things. JoAnn has a selection of rolling carts, most of which fold up when not in use, and many of them canvas-lined. The keys to success in happy green walking are to be prepared and to always have a good bag handy. We also have our bicycles and tricycles, and let me tell you: the tricycles rock. Best way to go shopping ever. Trust your Uncle Chippie on that one.

Most of our shopping excursions use one or more of the above. We might throw a bag or two in the back of a trike and head off for the grocery store. We even have insulated shopping bags for bringing home the cool stuff, and keep it cool en route. I really enjoy taking my trike up to the big orange hardware store, as they thoughtfully provided a good bike rack right out front. I try to support businesses that do that.

Then again, it doesn't hurt to have good shoes and to always wear socks. Now, when I say "good shoes," I don't mean you have to go out and buy really expensive, name-brand walking shoes. Because of all the cycling I do, I tend to wear inexpensive sneakerish-style shoes that fasten with Velcro instead of shoelaces. Those Velcro straps never come untied and get caught in the chain. I like that. Those shoes also work well for walking, an added bonus there. Wear shoes that you find to be comfortable when you walk a lot. You might not need the most expensive shoes on the market, but you will want comfortable shoes. And don't forget: always wear a good, thick pair of socks. They help a lot.

As for belt packs and backpacks, yes, we have a few. (Please don't ask me how many — I'd have to go count them.) Look for belt packs with wide belts, to keep them from cutting into your waist. Look for backpacks with padding in the panel that rests against your back, to keep the stuff in the pack from digging into your back. Also, a sternum strap is a nice touch. That's a strap that connects the two shoulder straps across your chest. That helps keep the straps from slipping off of your shoulders when

Are you ready to walk?

you walk, and it helps keep the backpack securely in place when you're on a bicycle. JoAnn and I both have backpacks close to the door, ready to be snatched at a moment's notice as we head out on an errand. We are always ready to walk.

Ah, but what about the rain, you ask? I'm glad you asked that. Of course, we have an answer. Several, in fact: we have umbrellas, ponchos and capes (oh my!). If we set off on foot and it looks like dark clouds gathering, we grab an umbrella. It's that simple. If dark clouds are gathering and we can hear the rumbling of thunder, we stay home. We are not stupid, and don't you be stupid either. Every year, people down here get struck and killed by lightning. No matter how bad a day you might be having, lightning can make it worse. And probably your last. Do not mess with lightning. Seriously. Stay home. You don't need to go anywhere that bad.

If it's just a light, non-electric sort of rain shower, then an umbrella is the answer, especially in the summer, when it's warm and humid. Ponchos and rain capes tend to hold in the warmth and leave you as wet from sweat as you would have been from the rain. Maybe more so. And a word to the wise: go for an umbrella with a "shepherd's crook" sort of handle, so you can hang it on your arm while you fumble with your keys and things. A real plus there. Enjoy the rain. It can be fun. Splish splash!

We also do walk in the dark. In the winter, we walk in the dark a lot, as the sun goes down so much earlier and we have little choice in the matter. For walking at night, bright, bright colors are the way to stay safe. And let me tell you: you cannot possibly overdress for this. You can never be *too* bright. We often wear those bright lime-green windbreakers you see more and more these days, and they work great. Failing that, white, yellow and orange are the colors of choice. Red is surprisingly not as bright as you might think it would be at night. The easiest answer: white. Wear white. Brilliant, stark, bleached white. No patterns, no stripes, just white. You *will* be seen.

We also own reflective vests, and we often add those as well, along with baseball caps with LED lights built right into the visors. We bought them at the local hardware store, and they each have a small button battery pack on the back size-adjustment strap. The quick push of a toggle turns them on. These caps are great for letting other people (like car drivers) know you are there, and when you get home, they're perfect for helping you find the lock with that key, hands free, in the dark. Also, they beat having to carry a heavy, cumbersome flashlight, which is another option. We prefer the light-up caps. They come in bright red, by the way. (Yes, I know: white would be better.) Find yourself a white shirt, a reflective vest, and a light-up red ball cap, and you are good to go out at night, on foot.

I think I should say something here about security issues when it comes to walking at all, and certainly when it comes to walking at night. In all of the years we have been out there, walking and cycling and all, we have never had a problem. But I know that doesn't mean I won't have a problem later today. We live in the middle of suburbia, and it *seems* safe. Still, we are always cautious and conscious of where we are and what's going on all around us. Didn't that car just pass us? Have we seen that guy before? Hear that car behind us? Is it slowing down? Turn now. Be ready.

I keep thinking I should carry a whistle, but honestly, what sort of defense is that? When it comes down to it, I can yell quite loudly and that's just as effective. And besides, I can yell words

I can't whistle. Quite loudly, if I have to. Don't make me go all thesaurus on you.

Fair warning right here: I will not tell you what JoAnn does for self-defense when she is out walking or riding her bicycle. It's none of your business unless you make it so, and then, all I can say is this: you'll be sorry. Never, ever, reveal every card in your hand. Always save the surprise.

Only walk where you feel safe, and only *when* you feel safe. If you set off from home and get *that feeling*, turn right around and go home. Don't like the way it looks that way? Go another way. Not sure about what's going on up ahead? Find another way to get there. Can't? Then don't. Go back, go home, and try again another day. If you aren't having fun, and this isn't fun, then don't do it. You don't need to get all stressed out over it, and you certainly don't need to put yourself in danger. This is all about living green, not pushing daisies. Stay safe. Please.

I've saved the best for almost last because this is a subject very near and dear to my heart: the bicycle. Specifically, practical bicycling. When it comes to living small and going green, nothing does all that the bicycle can do, and it can do all of that and more. Once you get past the energy and resources used to manufacture the bicycle and get it to the consumer, the bicycle is about as green as it gets. I don't know of any other device that saves money, energy and resources, reduces pollution, and helps keep you fit and happy, all at the same time. If you can name anything else that does all that, I'd like to hear about it. Daniel Behrman called the bicycle "the noblest of man's inventions," and I think he was absolutely right. So let's talk about that noble bicycle.

Earlier this year I wrote an entire book on the subject of practical bicycling. It was called, oddly enough, *The Practical Cyclist*.

Go figure. If, after reading what I have to say here, you want to know even more, then, yes, you might want to find a copy of that book. I'm just saying. Now let's talk bikes.

I'm not going to tell you about bicycle racing here. We're not going to go into the details of planning an epic long-distance bicycle tour or how to restore your father's antique Schwinn. This isn't about that. This is about riding your bicycle instead of driving your car. This is about making short trips on your bicycle around town. Nothing too difficult. Easy rides around to the neighbor and to the local store. Maybe, if you're really lucky, to work. This is about riding a normal, everyday bike, your bike, just a few miles at a time, instead of driving your car those few miles every time. You can do this. Trust me.

Chip's little bike shop

And let me say this right now, right up front: motor-assisted bicycles are a bad idea. If you've come to this book looking for justification for buying a motor-assisted bicycle, you are going to be very disappointed. It doesn't matter if we're talking about bicycles with batteries and electric motors here or bicycles with gas engines bolted to them. Either one is a bad idea. I'd say don't get me started, but since I am, hang on.

First off, there's a very good chance that these things aren't even legal where you live. That means not legal to ride in the street, not legal on the sidewalk, and most certainly not legal on any recreational trail. I find it somehow perversely ironic that they can even be sold, when they are not legal to use anywhere other than, say, in your own driveway. If you buy one of these, there's a very good chance you'll not be able to use it anywhere. Is that enough to scare you off? If not, read on.

The lack of legality aside, motor-assisted bikes are bad ideas from other angles as well. Gas or electric, you're still using energy and resources when the whole point is to not. They are, oddly enough, a sort of self-created need. That is, you need the motor assist because you have it. If you didn't have it, you wouldn't need it. Let me explain. The additional weight of the motor (gas or electric), along with the weight of the batteries or gasoline, all conspire to make your bicycle much heavier than it would be without all of this extra stuff. So, because you have all of that, you need all of that to move your now much heavier bicycle. (All of that extra weight makes it much harder to pedal when the motor's not on.) If you stripped off the motor, batteries or gas tank, the bike would be much lighter, and the motor assist unneeded. Problem solved.

So here's the bottom line: if you want to live small and go

green with a bicycle (and you should), then, yes, by all means, go green with a real bicycle, but not a motor-assisted mistake. Please. I'm begging here. Thank you.

Alright, now that I've got that out of my system, let's talk about *real* bicycles! The first question you'll probably want to ask is this: how much can I do by bicycle? The answer has to be this: a lot more than you think. There are many people across North America, and more every day, who are finding that they can do *everything* by bike. They are surprised to find that they really don't need a car to do all they want to do. Now, I'm not saying everyone can do that, but just about everyone is finding out that we can all do more by bicycle, and less by car. Ah, but how much more?

In the summer of 1976 I crossed America, from Reedsport, Oregon, to Yorktown, Virginia, on a bicycle. It took 81 days and over 4,200 miles (6,700 km), but I did it. (Thank you, Bike-Centennial!) I was younger then. I have covered 100 miles (160 km) in one day, with my best time being 5½ hours on a tandem. Again: younger then. Still, these days, I routinely ride ten and twenty miles a day, either for shopping, to run errands, or just for fun. Oddly enough, the longer mileage is more often just for fun. And it *is* fun. But what about you? What sort of distances can you expect to cover, comfortably, on a bicycle?

I would say, for the average person, you should be able to ride a bicycle to anything within three miles (5 km) of your home in complete comfort. I ride three miles one way to work and back every day. It takes me about twenty minutes, and I never hurry. I have coworkers who ride eight miles (13 km) to work one way, and they have no problem at all with that distance. How about we average it out? Let's say five miles (8 km), one way, is a very good, realistic limit to practical bicycling here in suburbia. Your mileage, as they say, may vary.

There can, of course, be real physical (geographical) limits to your local, practical bicycling no matter where you are. Hills, highways, railroad tracks and water all tend to stop smaller roads from going through. It can be frustrating when you're trying to get from Point A to Point B, and River C stops Road D from going through because no one could justify building Bridge E. (C'est la vie.) Maybe I can help.

Just as with walking, start with making a list of everywhere you'd like to ride your bicycle. You'll probably be surprised about how much there really is within five miles of your home. Not sure how far out that five-mile limit might be? Start with this: Lay out a good street map of where you live. Mark your home on the map. Now, with a compass, draw a big circle around your home, but with a three-mile radius. Not five. Three. Why three? Because a three-mile radius becomes five miles of bicycling as you take the connecting, right-angled streets to zigzag out to that three miles limit. Welcome to Uncle Chippie's Pythagorean Theorem of Practical Cycling. Three'll get you five when it comes to riding across town. Of course, that works for kilometers as well, but give yourself a five-kilometer radius for about an eight-kilometer cycling distance through town — it's about the same. There you go. Well, not quite yet. We still have work to do here.

Once you get your limits in place, you're going to want to look at a good topographical map. (I didn't want you to mess up your topo map with that big three-mile circle.) Topographical maps have light contour lines that show you where all the hills are, how tall they are, and how steep they are. This is the map that will help you get around the hills, or at least find a way to maybe tackle the lower hills instead. See all of those thin contour lines swooping around all over? The object of this game is to get where you want to go by crossing the fewest number of lines. Fewer lines mean fewer hills. Yes, if you start and finish at home, you have an elevation gain of zero by the time you get back, but if you can avoid climbing hills either way, that will help, too.

The closer the contour lines are together, the steeper the hill. If you see a road going through a lot of contour lines all bunched together, that's a steep hill, either up or down. (You can check the

So many ways to not drive a car!

elevation numbers on the map to figure out what you're in for there.) Either way, you might want to avoid that road if you can. And that brings up the Zen Bicycle Hill Question: how far out of your way will you go to avoid a hill? Each of us has a different answer to that question, much like to this one: would you choose the short, steep hill or the longer, gentle one? To each their own. (I tend to attack the short, steep ones.) You're going to have to get out there and see what you're capable of and just how much you like climbing hills. Good luck with that, by the way.

Another booger when it comes to pedaling all over town is the increased dangers found on major roads. Please don't ride *on* the major roads. Use the smaller back roads instead. It's bad enough to just get *across* the big ones. You can use the topo map to find your way across major roads, but a general street map works just as well. Thanks to all of the driving you've been doing, you *know* where the major roads are. Now all you have to do is find the smaller roads that cross them. Preferably at a traffic light.

It's a sad fact of suburban life that very few small roads go all that far. If you get a few blocks out of one of them, consider yourself lucky. Larger roads, railroad tracks, and various bodies of water all tend to stop small roads in their tracks. We need to help you get around them and keep on going. For now, you need to play "Connect the Dots" to see if you can link small roads to get you where you want to go. Most of the time, you probably can, but maybe not always. Sometimes, you just can't get there from here. Sorry.

For now, as you get started, you might want to cross larger roads at small traffic light intersections. If you like, you can walk your bike across the wider roads. The idea is to use smaller roads, but you might have to use larger roads for short distances to get to those smaller roads. That's OK. That's all part of the fun, to see how far you can go and how you're going to get there.

There are, of course, other obstacles to your bicycling progress. Railroads and water (ponds, lakes, streams, rivers and oceans) are all out there, and all working to keep you home. Don't you let them. Your topo map will show the railroad lines in your town, but a general street map might not. Railroads are reluctant to let absolutely every road cross their tracks, so you might have to do some detouring to get across the tracks. A few minutes spent studying a good map now will save you both heartache and miles on the road later.

The same can be said for those larger bodies of water out there. Not every road is worth a bridge, and it can be difficult to find smaller bridges, or big bridges that are bicycle-friendly. Again, you have to study the map, know what's out there, and maybe make a few exploratory rides to see what's *really* out there for you and your bicycle. You are about to get to know your hometown in a detail you never thought possible.

Once you figure out where you can go, you have to figure out how to get there. Much of what I said about walking in the rain and walking in the dark also applies to bicycling in the rain and bicycling in the dark. You can get, and I do recommend, rain capes designed specifically for bicycling. These are waterproof capes with no armholes, but with loops that fasten over your brake levers in the front and with a loop to go around your waist to hold the cape down as you ride. They work great and can be had in bright colors for cycling on dark, rainy days. I carry one all the time. Cheap plastic ponchos that fasten down the side don't work so well on a bicycle. They aren't cut or made for the riding position and blow all over the place. Avoid them if you can when you ride your bike. You'll be glad you did. Also, if you're going to ride in the rain on a regular basis, you want fenders. Really, really good fenders. That makes a huge difference in the rain when it comes to keeping you dry. Umbrellas don't work so well on a bicycle, especially when it's windy. Fair warning there.

It might not rain every day, but it does get dark every night. (Well, it does where I live, anyway.) Yes, you can ride your bike at night, and I do spend a large part of the year riding to work in the early morning in the dark. Much like with walking in the dark, the key to safety and success here is to see and be seen. This means using lights on your bicycle, wearing bright clothing, and using reflectors on both. When I pedal to work in the dark, I use three LED (Light Emitting Diode) headlights and three LED taillights. LED lights are very bright, use little power, and are vibration-proof to get you through the rough spots without failing. I also wear a bright high-visibility lime-green windbreaker and have reflectors on everything. I go in for the rolling disco inferno look, and it's worked well for me so far.

Don't forget to add a brightly colored bicycle helmet and cycling gloves to your lovely cycling ensemble. The bicycle helmet gives you much needed visibility at car-driver height and helps you be seen in traffic as well as be identified as a cyclist (and not just some sort of fast-moving lump). Bicycle gloves (usually fingerless) will help keep your fingers from going numb and give you the padding and protection you're going to be glad you had if you ever come off that bike and land palms first. And you will land palms first. Everyone does.

Now let's work on that bicycle of yours. Let's make it more practical, more green, and more in tune with living small. Let's see if we can leave the car at home, just a little bit. To do that, your bicycle is going to have to do some things your car does, mainly, carry stuff. Not a lot of stuff, mind you, just a little. And we can do that.

While I do occasionally wear a backpack when I ride a bicycle, it is far more comfortable not to do so. That means you're going to want something on your bike to carry small packages and things you pick up along the way (like, when you go shopping). This is the whole point of using your bicycle instead of your car, right? For most people, and most bikes, that means adding some sort of basket.

Front baskets are the traditional way to carry a few small things, and they do work well, as long as those things are small. Too much weight up front can make for wonky steering, and nobody wants that. There are a lot of new front baskets on the market these days that feature some sort of quick-release mounting system, allowing you to take the basket off of the bike and take it with you into the store when you go shopping. I like that a lot. We have one, and JoAnn uses it all the time.

The classic wire saddle baskets, mounted on the back of the bike, carry a lot more, but you have to be more careful about packing them, as you can't see them all as you ride. It's very embarrassing to get home with empty saddle baskets after leaving the store with full ones. I hate it when that happens. Also, they don't usually come off the bike easily, if at all. Still, if you want to carry more, this might be the answer. Some of them do fold up flat when not in use, and that can be a plus when you don't need them.

The urban-chic answer to carrying things on a bicycle these days is a messenger bag, but I've had little luck with them myself.

They don't hold all that much, and if you really stuff them (as much as they can be stuffed), they tend to slide around as you ride. That can wreak havoc with your balance. Not good. If you want to avoid baskets on your bicycle, go with a small backpack and learn your limits when it comes to loading it. And do get one in a very bright color. That will help you be seen. It's all about visibility, even when it's not.

I mentioned fenders and lights earlier, and I have to say: that's what makes any bike a better, more practical bike. That's what makes your bike green and allows you to live small. On many of my bikes (and, yes, I have many) I've added a plastic milk-jug mud flap to the back bottom of the front fender. That keeps water from splashing on my shoes if I go through a puddle. Dry shoes make for happy feet. I prefer the classic, long, full fenders as opposed to the trendy short fenders that really don't do all that much to keep you dry. If your bike didn't come with fenders, this is where a little bit of money invested goes a long way toward making your bike a better choice. Get good fenders.

The same can be said for lights. If you can ride your bike at night, safely and legally, you might be more inclined to do so and leave the car at home for those short trips. Think of a night-time bicycle ride as being dark green. (Small joke there.) (Sorry.) You can get generator lights or battery-powered lights, even lights that use both. Legally, you have to have lights on your bike to ride it at night, probably both a head light and a taillight. Do it right, and riding at night can be a wonderful experience. Do it wrong, and you'll pedal into the nearest pothole after dark. Let's not.

One last must-have accessory to make your bicycle work as an alternative to the automobile: a good lock. A *really* good lock.

A good lock is what separates the cyclists from the pedestrians. A lousy bicycle lock (or none at all) will make you a pedestrian in fairly short order and with no warning.

Some years ago I built up a fixed-gear bicycle for my brother-in-law, Cecil. These are very odd bikes, in that they never coast at all, but once you get used to it, it's the most addicting ride in town. He loves his and rides it all over down on St. Pete Beach. He stopped one day to run into a local convenience store to get a drink. He did not lock the bike. (He was only going to be a minute, right?) When he came back out, the bike was gone. *Gone!* He looked around and spotted the bike about a block away on the ground. He walked over, picked it up, and rode home. What happened? We figured whoever swiped the bike jumped on it, pedaled like mad to get away, and then tried to coast. When they did that, when they tried to coast, the fixed-gear aspect of the machine threw them right over the handlebars. It'll do that.

We do not all ride fixed-gear bikes, and not all bikes will throw the thief off in such spectacular fashion. (Wouldn't that be great?) For now, for you, start with a good lock, one that uses a cable or chain to go through both wheels and the frame. Use it every time you stop and leave the bike somewhere, no matter how long you think you're going to be. Even for a minute. A bicycle can be stolen in less time than it takes to write this sentence. Or this one.

I try to only shop where I know I can lock up my bike safely and legally, without leaving it in anyone's way. That usually means locked in a bicycle rack, but not every business offers one. (If you want them to, ask them.) Don't leave your bike in the way by the front door. You won't like what you find when you get back. And only lock your bike to seriously immovable objects. Small trees do not count. Never let your bike get away. It can be a long walk home.

And always obey the law when you ride your bicycle. I know that sounds like a stupid thing to have to say, but you'd be amazed at how many people don't even know that there *are* a whole set of laws out there just for riding a bicycle. It's not the Wild West out there. Not even out west. Do check with your local law enforcement agency and see if there might be a few laws on the books about bicycling that could catch you off guard if you ride one.

Briefly, it often comes down to this: if the motor traffic in your part of the world drives on the right, then you ride your bicycle on the right, with that traffic. Never, ever ride against the flow of traffic. I know you might think it's a good idea because it lets you see what's about to hit you, but — you will get hit. Let's see if we can avoid that.

Obeying the law means obeying the law, and that means that, even on a bicycle, you have to stop for the red lights and stop, really stop, for the stop signs. Just as though you were in a car. The same laws apply to a bicycle. Don't be rude and run the red light or stop sign. Drivers hate it when you do that, and they're driving something much bigger than you. They can get a bit testy if provoked, and no one wants that. Stop when you should stop.

Also, here's a fun one: no headphones. No ear buds, no mugger magnets. Walking or cycling, you do want to hear everything that's going on all around you. You can hum a little tune in your head if you like, but please don't wear earphones. In many places (like here) it is illegal to wear headphones when you ride a bicycle. Even if it were legal, it would be a bad idea. Know the laws where you are, and always obey them, every time.

Whether you're walking or riding, it pays to always know where you are and where you're going. Nothing worse than that momentary panic as you go through an intersection and wonder, "Should I have turned there?" Too late now. Just go on through and turn at the next one. Always know where you are. Memorize those maps and know where you're going. Know what streets you want to be on and what streets to look for as you go. I'm famous for making small, hand-drawn maps to bring along with me, just in case. I still get lost, mind you, but at least I have a map to help me get back on track. Theoretically.

Never ride your bike on the same roads you'd take if you were driving. Look for the smaller, slower back roads, even if it means you're not taking the shortest route to where you want to go. Residential back roads are a much better ride on a bicycle than busy main thoroughfares. This is about safety, certainly, but it's also about having a nice time when you go out for a bicycle ride. If you don't enjoy riding your bicycle, you're not going to want to do it more often, and this is all about that. Find the road less traveled — it can make all the difference.

Avoid the major roads, and by all means avoid the major intersections. I know, sometimes you can't, but when you can, do. By planning ahead and using detailed maps, you should be able to do the vast bulk of your bicycling on quiet back streets and get where you want to safely and pleasantly. No one wants to see a harried green freak show up at their shop all tussled and flustered. Find the small roads and use them.

And what about riding your bicycle on the sidewalk? Before we move on here, we need to talk about that. For many people, especially people who haven't ridden a bicycle for a while (like, since the day you got your driver's license, right?), sidewalk riding offers a glimmer of seemingly safe hope in an otherwise motorized world. That said, I must say this: it's not all that safe, and it might not even be legal where you are. Do, definitely, check with local law enforcement before you set off on a bicycle on the sidewalk. Sidewalk riding presents a whole new set of dangers: drivers often won't see you at all, and now you have to yield to pedestrians on the same sidewalk. It is not always worth the effort.

Where I live, sidewalk bicycle riding is legal, but I do it sparingly. It works best on sidewalks that have no, or very few, driveways across them. It's at its worst in commercial districts where every business has at least two driveways across the sidewalk, and no driver is looking for you on any sidewalk. They just want to get in or out, and woe be unto anyone, on foot or on bike, who gets in their way. Don't let that be you.

You have the right to the road, and in almost every case, it's a good idea to take it. Under special circumstances, yes, the sidewalk might work, but most of the time the road is where you want to be. Most of the time, the road is safer. Again, do check with local law enforcement on the legality of sidewalk riding where you live before you ride on the sidewalk.

Living small, being green, and riding your bicycle all boils down to organizing that smaller monkeysphere. It's all about getting your life down to a manageable level, one where you can actually go ride your bike instead of being stuck in your car every time you want to go someplace. Nothing you do will make you feel as good about what you do as riding your bicycle. It's the very best feel-good green in town. This is where you save money, save energy, conserve resources, lower pollution *and* keep yourself healthy and happy. One bike does it all. Wow!

As with so much of what I talk about here, start small and work your way up from there. Maybe go for short bicycle rides in your neighborhood before you work your way up to a ride to the local store. Get comfortable with your bike and be comfortable on the roads near your home before you branch out and try further roads and (relatively) distant destinations. No, you might not be able to go everywhere on your bike, but I suspect you will be amazed at how far you can go.

And hey, keep your bike tires pumped.

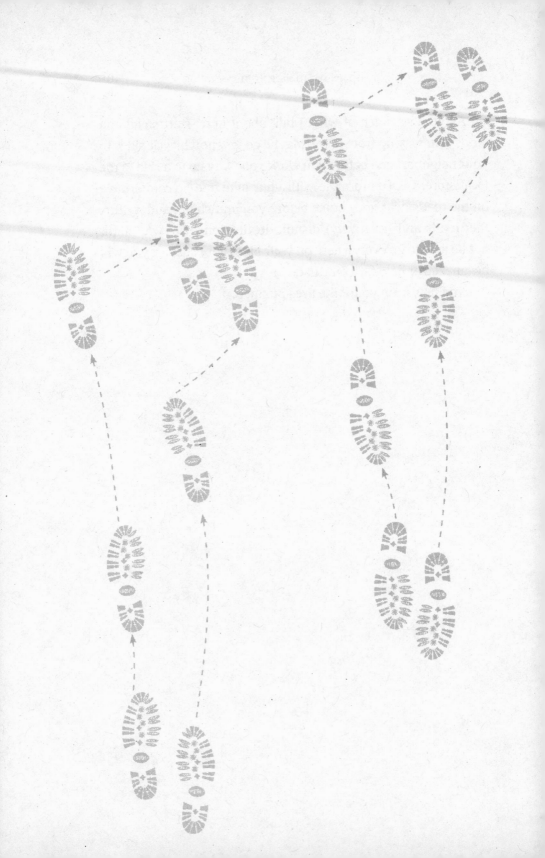

9

The Big, er, Small Finish

WEARING SMALLER SHOES (living small and being green) is all about getting by without being a total pig about it. It's very easy to be a pig. We're all pigs about something, every last one of us. Yes, even me. Oink. You just have to learn to be a slightly smaller pig. As I said right from the start, it's not about doing less, it's about doing what you do *with* less. I don't use nearly the amount of energy and resources I did ten years ago, and yet I'm still out there, doing it all. I just do it using a little bit less. Now it's your turn.

Living small is all about finding an easy green routine and getting used to living your life that way. In one way, it can be a very radical approach to living in suburbia (as we do), but, on the other hand, it's the kind of life we will all, eventually, have to lead, whether we like it or not. I think it's better to get a jump on the future and try on those smaller, greener shoes before they're the only ones in the store. I'm glad we started doing all of this some years ago, and we're still out there looking for new ways to go smaller and live greener. And you know what? It's still fun. I mean that.

You can do this, too. I've tried hard not to make this sound like some vast and complex undertaking that would terrify someone to even contemplate. It's not. It's easy. You can do it. The key to living small is to start small. Don't try to do it all at once, or even to do a lot of it at once. Pick something, just one thing, that tickles your fancy and give it a go. Maybe change out a few old incandescent light bulbs for the new low-energy CFLs. That's a great way to start. Very easy to do. Maybe you could go and check out the local recycling center. Ride your bicycle around the block. You don't even have to tell your neighbors that you're thinking about this. It will be our little secret. I'm not going to sneak over one night and put a big sign in your front yard that says, "HEY, THESE PEOPLE ARE GOING GREEN! HA!" You can do anything you want, including doing nothing at all. But then, anyone can do nothing, and most people do.

JoAnn and I got to where we are today by starting small at living small. We have, over time (over years), made small changes in almost everything we do. I would be hard pressed to name one aspect of our lives that has not changed for the smaller, or greener, as it were. One small thing gets changed, then another. We never did try to change too much at once, and the outcome has been very satisfying, even if it has taken years to get to where we are now. And we are still working on it, still changing things, one (small) thing at a time, year after year.

Has our daily routine changed all that much as we have gotten smaller and greener? I want to say no, but small changes over time are hardly noticed, and maybe it all has added up to big changes in our lives. Maybe the big picture is radically different for us these days, compared to, say, twenty years ago. I still get up every morning, have breakfast, and go to work. That hasn't changed. Yes, I ride my bicycle to work these days, but that's what I do. That's just me. I'm very lucky to be so close to work that I can ride my bike, and by doing so, I'm saving a lot of money. We do not sit in the dark and weave paper hats from old newspapers. (We recycle those old newspapers instead!) We do not exist in a hollow world of stark self-denial. We're too busy having fun.

So why would anyone want to even try to do this? Why live small and go green? Let's get really crass about this and talk money here. I know, I know, it's all about saving the planet and small furry woodland creatures. What. Ever. Get over it. You want the bottom line? Here's an idea of what the bottom line is for us, keeping in mind that it is just the two of us.

My riding a bicycle to work saves us the expense of a second car. That's $8,000 a year right there. Nice start, huh? We use one fifth of the regional average when it comes to electricity in our home. Our power bill is just over $30 a month, so we're saving about $120 a month over the average bill. There's another $1,440 a year in savings. Ca-ching! With all of the recycling we do, we're saving a cool $500 in not needing curbside garbage pickup. *Sweet*. Our lowered water use all around the house (and yard) probably saves us another $180 a year. Not much savings there, comparatively, but no small change either. Just those four items right there save us over ten thousand dollars a year. That would be 10,000 reasons to go green and live small, would it not? I think so. And, yes, we could do more. Maybe a lot more, depending on how radical we wanted to go. For now, this is good. I'm happy with where we are. Our shoes are small enough.

There are also some good health reasons for living small and going green. I had been riding my bicycle for quite some time before we got all green about it, and let me tell you: adding walking to my daily routine helped me shed fifty pounds. No joke. Fifty pounds. Could you stand to lose a few pounds? Try going green. That'll do it. Just getting out and walking and riding your bicycle a little bit will make you feel much better. The fresh air will do you good. A little added exercise around the house, even if all you're doing is going out to the garage to pitch something in the recycle bin, is always a good thing. Don't just sit there. Get up and do something green!

There's also a certain healthy mental aspect to this. It feels good, mentally, to do this. Living small will give you a whole

Green is cool. Trust me.

new outlook on life and make you feel as though you're doing the right thing. Yes, you *are* doing the right thing, but this time it even feels like it. There's a lot to be said for having the right attitude, and this will give you that. Want to feel better about yourself and your life? I think we've got the answer right here: go a little green. Want to feel even better? Go a lot green.

Of course, there's always the idea of doing something good for the environment. I won't say that's not an overused cliché, but we do seem to get bombarded with it a lot these days. Seems like every TV commercial and advertisement these days is all about how green the latest flapdoodle is. There's a lot of greenwashing out there, and it can be tough to tell when you really *are* doing something good for the planet. How do you know what to buy? Hint: buying a car, any car, is not doing something good for the planet. I don't care what the guy in the car commercial told you. Living small means living your life with less impact on the world around you. That means buying less. That means using less energy and fewer resources. Leaving a smaller footprint means wearing smaller shoes. No way around it. If you need less and you buy less, you use less — and that helps. It really does. Green, really green, is good for the world around you, starting with your home and yourself.

Then again, you need to know this: there's a good chance your personal reputation is going to take a real hit with this one. Can you handle it? Start swapping out light bulbs and throw a couple of bins out in the garage for newspapers and plastics, and watch your friends and neighbors look at you funny. Hey, you've gone all green! All weird. All hippy-dippy. Can your reputation handle that sort of change? Can you live up to your new green image? Our small changes over time have still led us to a much different life compared to, say, that of our neighbors. I do not run a big lawn tractor over my yard every week whether it needs it or not. We do not water the lawn every day, spend our weekends fertilizing it and making it look like a golf course. We have trees and we live in the woods. That's our image. It's how we live. We do not have two big SUVs in the garage. We have a garage full of bicycles and tricycles and one lone truck that we *use* as a truck. Could you live like that? Would you even want to be known as "the bicycle person" in your neighborhood?

True story: some time ago, a woman drove from 25 miles (40 km) away to have me work on her husband's bicycle. She did not know my name and only had a vague description of where I lived. She got within half a mile or so of our house and was lost. She pulled over and asked a couple of kids if they knew where the bicycle guy lived. They led her straight to me. Do you want a reputation like that? Can your family survive being "the Greenies"? If you think you can take it, then this just might be the life for you. Living small is cool.

On the other hand, you *can* take this green thing too far. It's easy to do. (Or so I've been told.) That hippy-dippy earth-shoe image is out there, just waiting to latch onto the next person who jumps in too deep. Wade in cautiously, and always be aware of how far you've gone. It's too late for us. Save yourself. How do you know if you've gone too green?

* If you're so used to wandering around in your house without turning on a light that you forget where the light switches are, you've gone too green. Take a step back.
* You look at your key ring and wonder what that odd key is, and it turns out to be the one for the car? Yeah, you've gone green. Deep green.

* Ever pulled a loose thread off a piece of clothing and wondered what recycle bin it goes in? Can you feel the green in this room?
* Have you ever contemplated putting a CFL bulb in the fridge? Yeah, you could be the next mayor of Green City. (And I have to say, yes, I've honestly thought about that one.)
* Did you grow a beard to save energy and resources? And then grew it longer to save more? Oh, you are one seriously green dude. What's that? You're not a dude? Whoa! Too much information! Too much information!

All you gotta do is pitch in.

All things in moderation, Grasshopper. You don't need to transform yourself into a total green freak overnight. Small steps and little changes do add up over time, and you want to give yourself a chance to get used to every small change as you try them on for size. Only go as far as you want to go, and at your own pace. You can chart your progress with those lower energy bills and use the money saved to get yourself further down the road to Green City. Or at least into the suburbs, where we are.

Somewhere along the line, as you make these green changes in your life, you'll look at how other people live their energy-intensive lives and wonder if you were ever like that. That's when you know you've made the change. Welcome to the world of living small. You're there.

I look at how we live our lives even now, and I still see room for change. There's still room for improvement. We could live a little smaller. A little greener. Maybe a lot smaller, if we were willing to make bigger changes. For now, I'm happy with our somewhat green-ish lives in the middle of this endless suburbia. It's always good to have room to grow, to have more goals (green or otherwise) to shoot for. And we will always have those. Welcome to my world.

Index

Page numbers in italics refer to photographs.

A
"above-ground factors," 17
acquisitions, need *vs.* want, 24–25, 33,
    123
appliances
  clothes dryers, 69, 70, 71
  dishwashers, 45, 51, 102
  Energy Star, 51
  microwaves, 44, 45
  refrigerators, 45, 51
  replacement of, 64
  stoves, 44
ash, fireplace, 32
awnings, 84

B
backpacks, 147–48
batteries
  chargers, 29
  disposal of, 29, 31
  dry cell, 29
  electric car, 129
  heavy electric bicycle, 39, 152
  powered from, 30
  rechargable, 29, 30, 31
  rechargeable systems, 29–30
Begley Jr., Ed, 8, 33, 34, 35, 56, 58
Behrman, Daniel, 150
belt packs, 147
best of both worlds, 51
"bicycle recycle" T-shirts, *3, 8,* 28–29,
    170, 183
bicycles
  buses, on, 140–41
  electric, 39–40, 152
  fixed-gear, 161
  folded, 141
  green, as, 6, 150, 153
  motor-assisted, 152
  salvaging, 27–28
  "the noblest of man's inventions," 150
  tubes
    handlebar tape, as, *25,* 26–27

  wheel spokes
    hangers, as, 27
bicycling, practical
  accessories
    carrying, 159–61
    fenders, 158, 160
    lights, 158, 160
    locks, 160–61
  back roads and major roads, 156, 163
  clothing
    night, 158
    rain, 157
  comfortable distances, 126, 153, 154
  destinations, 129, 154
  driving, *vs.*, 19–20, 142, 151, *155*
  exploratory rides, 157
  geographical limits, 154–56
  green, as, 142, 150, 164
  hearing what's around you, and, 162
  keeping your tires pumped, 165
  knowing where you are, 163
  laws, obeying the, 162
  locks and locking up, 160–61
  maps
    street, 154, 156, 157, 163
    topographical, 154–155, 156, 157
  obstacles, 157
  reasons for, 19, 20, 170
  savings, and, 19, 169
  sidewalk riding, 163–64
  starting small, 165, 168
  Uncle Chippie's Pythagorean Theorem,
    154
bins
  recycling
    formal, for, 11, 31, 111, 112, 113, 120
    informal, for, 31, 32, 112, 117, 118
    local grocery store, at the, 35, 114
  regular trash, 123
bookmarks, 26
brooms *vs.* leaf blowers, *106,* 106–7
bus systems, municipal
  Bikes on Buses program, 140–41

folding bikes, and, 141
mass transit, available, *138,* 137

C
Cadillac V8 *vs.* Moto Guzzi V8, 131
cardigans, 81, 82
cars
    electric, 129–30
    engine options, 133
    gas or diesel, 132
    less use of, 142, 151, 153, 158, 159, 160
    Living Green Expo, at, 126
    microcars, 129–30
    need for, 128, 132
    second, expense of, 20, 169
    shopping tips, 130, 133
    See also vehicles
cell phones, 41, 76
    chargers, 47
CFLs
    innovation, as most important, 56
    lumens per watt, 58, 61, 62
    problems with, 57, 62
    quirks and differences
        color, 59
        heat, lack of, 59–60
        initial dimness, 58
    savings with, 58
    sizes and styles, 56–57, 59, 61
changes
    small
        adusting to temperatures, 81
        big *vs.,* 4, 5
        over time, 4, 17, 18, 20, 168, 171
        savings, effecting, 39
        "unpowered," 80
chargers, battery, 29, 30, 76
clocks
    appliances, in, 43, 44, 45
    battery operated, advantages of, 46
    electric and electronic, 43–45
    in every room, 46
clothes dryers, 69, 70, 71
clotheslines, 70, 71
combustibles, recycling, 31, 32, 117, 118, 119, 120
compact fluorescent light bulbs. *See* CFLs
composting, 120–122
confessions, 40–42
conserving. *See* saving
credit cards, reusing, 26

curtains, 52, 85, 103
Cycles and recycles, all in one, 5
cylinders, engine, 130–31

D
diesel, 129, 132
dishwashers, 45, 51, 102, 103
dishwashing
    Uncle Chippie way, the, 103
displacement, engine, 130–31, 133
doorbells, 75–76
doors
    garage, 93
    storm, 88
    weather stripping, 87
draft dodgers, 87
drying clothes, 69–71

E
eaves, wide, 84
Ed Begley Jr., 8, 33, 34, 35, 56, 58
electric bills. *See* power bills
electric cars, 129–30
electric *vs.* electronic, 46–47
electricity
    average suburban use, 38
    bills
        lowering the, 11, 12, 38–39, 42–43
        kilowatt-hours, 38
        lower use *vs.* increased technology, 39, 69
electricity, saving
    artificial lighting, through
        CFLs, using, 58
        fewer lights, using, 54
        LEDs, using, 62
    clothes dryer use, less, 69–71
    Energy Star products, using, 50–52
    natural light, using, 52–53, 103
    power strips, using, 48, 49
    substituting battery-power, by, 44, 46
    unplugging, by, 43–45
    water heating systems, through
        solar, 68–69
        tank size and insulation, 65
        tankless systems, 67–68
        thermostat, lowering the, 66–67
        timers, 65
electronic items
    battery charging stations, 75, 76
    glowing power lights, 48
    "off," meaning of, 47, 75

power drain solutions
Energy Star electronics, 51
power strips, 48–49, 73
toys, fewer, 49–50
electronic *vs.* electric, 46–47
Energy Star, 50, 51–52
engines
cylinders, number of, 130–31
cylinders *vs.* displacement, 131
diesel, 132
displacements, 130–31, 133
gasoline, 12, 132
options, 133

F
Farnsworth, Philo T., 72
faucets, 99, 100, 108
flues, fireplace, 88–89, *89*
fluorescent lights. *See* CFLs
formal recycling, 31, 110, 111. See also
recycling: formal
four Rs
applying the, 33
poetic green reality, as, 35
recycle, 31–33
reduce, 23–25
refuse, 33–35
reuse, 26–31

G
gadget freaks, electronic, 41–42
garage doors, 93
garbage
bills, *10,* 110, 169
curbside pickup, 109–10, 119, 169
landfills, 13
organization of, 118
overestimation of, 119
power plants, 13
small amounts of, 14, 109, 121, 123
glowing lights, 43, 48. See also "off"
golf carts, 133–34, 135
"go-peds," 136–37
gray water use. *See* laundry: water
green
bottom line, 169
buzz word, as new, 6
freaks, 4, 5, 12, 13, 163
going
fun, as, 18
health reasons for, 142, 170
images, 20, 32, 171, 172

innovations for living, 56
on purpose, 17
routines
glitch in the, 45
habits, getting into, 18
JoAnn's and Chip's, 18–20
over time, 2, 17, 167
pleasant and enjoyable, as, 100
recycling as part of, 31
streamlining the, 119
traveling (*See* traveling green)
greenwashing, 6, 171
"greeness," questioning, 7

H
handlebar tape
bicycle tubes as, 26–27
headphones, 162
hot water. *See* water heating systems
house, working with the existing
awnings, metal, 84
doors, 87, 88, 94–95
garage, 93
flues, fireplace, 88–89
insulation, 86–88, 90–92, 93
orientation
garage placement, 84
prevailing winds, and, 77–78
shade, for, 83, 84
sun, for, 89–90
windows, 78, 79, 84, 89–90, 92
roofs
ridge vents, 94
solar panels on *vs.* tree shade over,
40, 69
Hubbert, Marion King, 15
Hubbert's Peak, 15

I
identifying recyclables, 113
images, green, 20, 32, 171, 172
informal recycling, 31, 110, 111. See also
recycling: informal
insulation
attic, 90–92
cut, blocks, 91
liquid expanding foam, 91
loose, blown cellulose, 91
lunch box option for no, 92
garage doors, 93
home, 86, 90, 92
key, as, 90

tanks, hot water, 65, 66, 67
trapped air, 88

J
jalousie windows, 79, 80, 94, 95
jars, peanut butter, *25,* 27, 113
Jimmy Carter, President, 81, 82
jokes
    lame, 1
    no, 62, 142, 170
    semi-Amish, 41
    small, 66, 160

K
kilowatt-hours, 38

L
landfills, 9, 11, 13, 14, 29, 119
laundry
    full loads, 104
    water, 103, 105
leaks, water, 108
LEDs
    advantages, 62
    baseball caps with, 149
    bicycle lights, 61, 158
    disadvantages, 63
    lumens per watt comparisons, 62
    TLT, as, 61
    "warm white" buying tip, 62
light
    ambient, using, 52
    artificial, saving on, 52, 53–63
    daylight outside, using, 53
    natural, using, 52
    See also lighting
light-emitting diodes. *See* LEDs
lighting
    CFL, 56. See also CFLs
    LED, 61. See also LEDs
    motion sensors, 54
    night-lights, 55
    unnecessary, eliminating, 54
Living Green Expo, 63, 126
living small
    benefits of, 16, 21, 169
    concept of, 1, 12
    confessions re, 40–42
    health reasons for, 170–71
    just say no, 33

key to, the, 168
limbo, as a sort of, 129
    philosophy of, 23
    on purpose, 17, 167
    theme song, 35
    vs. living large, 9
    want to or not, 16
logo, recycling, 113
louvered windows, 79. See also jalousie
    windows
low-impact travel, 141
lumens per watt, 58, 61, 62

M
maps
    street, 154, 156, 157, 163
    topographical, 154–55, 156, 157
    walking and riding, for, 163
mass transit, 137
Mercedes Smart car, 129
Miami windows, 79
microcars, 129–30
modes of transportation
    downsizing, 129
    matching the machine to the trip, 127,
        128
money
    investing a little to save, 51, *56,* 71,
        87, 94
    measurement of savings, as, 2, 3, 9,
        11
    saved, as the bottom line, 169
    spending the savings, 4, 21, 174
monkeyspheres, 126, 164
motion sensor lights, 54
Moto Guzzi V8 *vs.* Cadillac V8, 131
motor oil, recycling, 116
motor scooters
    advantages and disadvantages, 135
    buying tips, 135–37
    Harley-Davidson Topper, 137
    matching the machine to the trip, 127
    motorcycles *vs.,* 136
motorcycles
    buying tips, 136
    matching the machine to the trip,
        127
    Moto-Guzzi V8, 131
    scooters *vs.,* 135
mugging magnets, 162

N

need *vs.* want, 25, 33, 35, 50, 123, 132
newspapers
    recycyling, 11, 31, 111
    start, the, 5, 10, 110
night-lights, 43, 44, 55, 72

O

"off," 47, 51, 75
oil
    by-products, 16
    food production, effects on, 16
    Hubbert's Peak, 15
    "oil production," 16
    production curve, 15
    recycling motor, 116
    supply and demand, 16, 17
    traveling alternatives to using, 141
    US production peak, 15
outdoor motion sensor lights, 54

P

phones, 41, 42, 76
"plastic pumpkins," 33
plastic shopping bags. *See* shopping bags:
    plastic
poetic green reality, 35
power bars. *See* power strips
power bills
    kilowatt-hour, as billed by the, 38
    lowering the, 43, 51
        clothesline, by using a, 71
        electricity, by using less, 24, 39
        figuring out your usage, by, 43
        hot water efficiency, through, 64, 66,
            67
        insulating, through, 88, 90, 91
        lightbulbs, by changing, 63
        power strip, by using a, 73, 75
        turning off lights, by, 54
        unplugging, by, 45, 46, 48, 76
        watching them closely, by, 42
    savings, JoAnn's and Chip's, 12, 169
power drains
    glowing lights, 43, 48
    montion sensor lights, 54
    phantom, *44,* 73, 75
    standby, the constant, 51, 75
    unchecked electronic, 49
power plants, 9, 13, 30, 50–51, 130

power strips
    audio systems, and, 74
    computer systems, and, 74–75
    convenience, 48, 49
    electronic power drain, and the, 49, 73
    TV systems, and, *47,* 48, 49, 51, 73–74
Publix supermarket, recycling bins, 114

R

rain gear, 148, 157–58
rainwater, collection, 107
Reagan, 81
recycling
    bicycles, 27–29
    bins, 11, 111, 114, 120
    buying tips, 32, 33
    centers, 11, 31, 111, 113, 116
    clean, 113, 115–16
    combustibles, 31–32
    formal, 31, 111–16
        batteries, 31
        corrugated cardboard, 113
        disposal, 114, 116, 120
        glass, 116
        metals, 114–15
        mixed paper, 111–12
        motor oil, 116
        newspaper, 111
        plastic shopping bags, 35, 113–14
        plastics, 113–14, 122
        Styrofoam, 113–14
    four Rs, as one of the, 23, 31–33
    images, 32, 109
    informal, 31, 111–22
        ash, fireplace, 32
        buying carefully, 121
        combustibles, 117–18
        composting, 120–21
        composting, in-ground, 121–22
        mulching lawn clippings, 111, 117
        tree limbs, 117
        yard waste, 32
    key to, 32
    marks, identifying, 113
    missteps and solutions, 118–20
    modern technology, as, 32
    percentage, JoAnn's and Chip's, 14, 109
    routines, 109, 111
    savings, 169
    systems, 32, 119, 120

washing the, 113, 115–16
water, of, 97, 104
reducing
  acquisitions, 24
  electrical use, 24
  four Rs, as one of the, 23–25
  need *vs.* want, 25, 33
  ten percent, by, 23, 24
  vehicle mileage, 24
  water use, 99
refusing
  four Rs, as one of the, 23, 33–35
  just say no, 33, 35
  "plastic pumpkins," 33
  plastic shopping bags, 33–35
reputation, 171, 172. See also image
resources
  bills, 21. See also power bills; water
    bills
  fewer, using, 1, 126, 142, 171
  non-renewable energy, 16
    electric vehicles, and, 129
    peaks and declines, 17
  saving, 2, 9, 109, 140, 150, 164
  saving money as measurement of
    saved, 11
  two-for-one savings, 105
reusable shopping bags, 34
reusing
  batteries, 29–31
  bicycle tubes, 26–27
  bicycle wheel spokes, 27
  bicycles, 27–29
  credit cards, 26
  four Rs, as one of the, 23, 26–31
  informal recycling, as, 31
  plastic items, 113
  purest form of recycling, 26
  scrutinizing the recycling, by, 27
  second nature, as, 27
rising prices, 17, 68, 135
roofs
  colors, 94
  cooled by shade trees, 82
  materials, 93, 94
  ridge vents, 94
  solar panels on *vs.* trees over, 40, 68,
    69
  White House, the, 81
  See also insulation: attic
routine, green. *See* green: routine

S
saving
  effort, 9
  environment, 9
  kilowatts, 38
  money, 2, 3, 9, 11, 169
  planet, the, 21, 169
  power, 2, 39, 42, 169
  price of this book, the, 2
  resources, 2, 9, 109, 140, 150, 164
  serious coin, 2
  small furry woodland creatures, 169
  "unpowered" changes, through, 80
  See also electricity: saving; water: using
    less
savings
  beard, of having a, 55
  bottom line, the, 169
  easy to see, 37
  Energy Star appliances, through, 51
  garbage bill, on the, 110, 169
  power bill, on the, 12, 38–39, 169
  two-for-one deal, a, 105
  unneeded second vehicle, on an, 20
  unplugging gizmos, through, 50
  water bill, on the, 169
shade
  awnings, 84
  coolant, as unpowered, 40, 69, 82, 95
  eaves, wide, 83–84
  solar panels, *vs.,* 40, 69
  trees, 40, 69, 82–83
shopping bags
  canvas, 34, 114, 146
  insulated, 146
  messenger type, 146, 159
  plastic, 33, 34, 35, 113, 146
  reusable, 34
showers
  baths *vs.,* 98
  friend, with a, 64, 98
  hot, civilized, 63, 68
  showerheads, low-flow, 99
  "the Navy way," 100, 101
  thermostat settings, and, 66
shredding mixed paper, 26, 112
shutters, 84
single-hung windows, 79, 94, 95
Smart car, Mercedes, 129
solar
  film, 84, 85

panels
  electric cars, 130
  photovoltaic, 130
  rooftop *vs.* shade, 40, 82
  White House, The, 81
power
  water heating, for, 68, 69
standby power drains, 51, 75
storm doors and windows, 88
Styrofoam, recycling, 114
supply and demand, 16, 17
swimming pools, 41
  saving electricity, 68, 107
  saving water, 107
  skateboard sales, and, 41
  Vatican, and the, 41
symbols, recycling, 113

T
technology
  diesel, 132
  LED, 61, 62, 63
  low-tech *vs.* high-tech, 2, 39, 69
  recycling as applied modern, 32
  unnecessary, 39, 40
televisions. *See* TVs
"The Forgotten Commodity," 97
thermostat settings, 66, 68, 81–82
TLT (the latest thing), 61
toilet paper, recycled, 7, 32
toilets
  low-flow models, 101, 102
  recycling rain water for, 107
  sanitizers, automatic, 102
  tanks, displacing water in, 101
toys
  electronic gadgets, as, 41
    battery charging stations, and, 75
    using fewer, 49–50
transportation
  downsizing, 129
  matching modes to needs, 127, 128
  See also bicycles; mass transit; tricycles;
    vehicles
trapped air, 88, 92
trash, 13, 24, 123
  See also garbage
traveling green, 125
  bus systems, municipal, 137
    Bikes on Buses program, 140–41
    general information needed, 137–40

choices, 129
combining trips, by, 127, 128
daily travel as discretionary, 125
defining needs, 128, 137
downsizing your vehicle, 128, 129, 133
eliminating the need for two vehicles,
  by, 130
engine displacement, through smaller,
  133
first rule of, 126
mass transit, 137
mode of transport, through, 127, 128,
  129
monkeysphere, 126, 164
options, low-impact, 141
using less energy and fewer resources,
  by, 126
See also bicycling; walking
trees
  hugging, *3,* 12, 21
  limbs, as combustibles, 32, 117, 118, 119
  planting, 2, 83, 84
  shade, providing, 40, 69, 82–83, 95
  trimming, 90
tricycles, 114, 127, 135, 145, 146
trucks
  engine displacement, 133
  functioning gasoline engine, as, 12
  gas or diesel, 132
  mode of transportation, as, 127
  needs for, examining, 130, 132–33
T-shirts, "bicycle recycle," 28–29
TVs
  Energy Star, 51
  flat screen *vs.* cathode ray tube, 72
  night-light, as, 72
  "off," and, 47
  power strip, and the, 48, 51, 73
    taping, reminder re, 74
  power usage, and, 72
  rumors re ownership, 49
  saving power, 72–73
twist ties, 27

U
Uncle Chippie
  trusting, 33, 65, 146
Uncle Chippie's
  Pythagorean Theorem of Practical
    Cycling, 154
  way to do dishes, 103

way to keep warm in the winter, 90
"unpowered" changes, 80

V
vehicles
  downsizing, 129–33
  electric, 129–30
  eliminating the second, 19, 130
  gas or diesel, 132
  golf carts, 133–34, 135
  greenest, 6
  greenwashing, 6
  microcars, 129–30
  motor scooters, 135–37
  motorcycles, 136
  needs for, examining, 130, 132–33
  shopping for, 130–131, 133
  See also bicycles; tricycles

W
walking
  barefoot, 6
  daily routines, 10, 114, 144, 170
  destinations, 127, 142
  distances, 126, 142, 143, 144
  driving, *vs.*, 142, 144
  gear
    carrying, 145–46, 147–48
    clothing
      after dark, 148–49
      footwear, 146–47
      rain gear, 148
    joys and benefits, 142, 143–44, 170
    key to successful, 144
    knowing where you are, 163
    maps, 163
    rates, 126, 143, 144, 145
    reasons for, 20, 145
    safe, feeling, 150
    security issues, 149
want *vs.* need, 25, 33, 35
water
  barriers to bicycling, as, 154
  bills, 98, 169
  leaks, checking for, 108
  rainwater, 97, 107
  supply, 97, 98
  tanks, 64, 65
  "The Forgotten Commodity," 97
  toxins leaching into, 29
  using less
    inside

    dishwashing tips, 103
    faucet aerators, low-flow, 99, 100
    flushing frequency, 102
    laundry tips, 103–104
    showerheads, low-flow, 99
    showering "the Navy way," 100
    toilet tanks, displacing water in, 101
    toilets, low-flow models, 101, 102
    turning taps, off and on, 100, 101
    washers, installing, 99
  outside
    drought-tolerant native plants, 105
    laundry gray water, 105
    pool covers, 107
    rainwater collection, 107
water heating systems
  circuit breakers, 66, 68
  solar, 68–69
  tank
    insulation, 65, 66, 67
    size, 64, 65
  tankless systems, 67–68
  thermostat settings, 66–67, 68
  timers, 64, 65, *65,* 67, 68
weather stripping, 87
Whimzy Whimsical House, 92
windows
  awnings, 84
  curtains, thermal, 85
  double pane, thermal, 94
  drafts, testing for, 88
  frames, color of, 92
  insulation
    around, 86, 87
    trapped air, 88
  jalousie, 79, 80, 94, 95
  louvered, 79
  Miami, 79
  open
    breeze, for, 85, 86
    hazards, 86
  oreintation, 84, 92
  sealing of, 88
  single-, double-hung, 79, 95
  solar film, 84, 85
  storm, 88
  trimming trees around, 90

Z
ZENN (Zero Emission, No Noise) microcars, 129

About the Author

CHIP HAYNES lives with his wife, the lovely JoAnn, in their mostly typical 1,500-square-foot, two-bedroom, two-bathroom suburban house in Pinellas County, Florida, right between Clearwater and Largo. Their two-car garage is full of bicycles and tricycles (and that one lone pickup truck), and their home is full of books. They have two rows of recycled theater seats in front of the TV and big green metal frogs bolted to the outside of the house. Their neighbors love them.

Having been where they are for as long as they have, Chip and JoAnn are very easy to find. They're in the phone book, or you can just pedal down Lake Avenue and look for those frogs. (The "Haynes Plaza" sign at the end of the garage driveway might be a bit of a tip-off.) In the evenings after their walk, Chip can often be found out in the garage working on bicycles.

New Society Publishers have been very kind to the fuzzy little green guy, and for that, he is eternally and internally (if not infernally) grateful. Any comments, complaints or compliments should be directed their way as well. They should know what you're thinking about all of this.

Living la vida verde!

If you have enjoyed *Wearing Smaller Shoes*, you might also enjoy other

Books to Build a New Society

Our books provide positive solutions for people who
want to make a difference. We specialize in:

Sustainable Living ✦ Ecological Design and Planning

Natural Building & Appropriate Technology ✦ New Forestry

Environment and Justice ✦ Conscientious Commerce

Progressive Leadership ✦ Resistance and Community

Nonviolence ✦ Educational and Parenting Resources

New Society Publishers

ENVIRONMENTAL BENEFITS STATEMENT

New Society Publishers has chosen to produce this book on recycled paper made with 100% post consumer waste, processed chlorine free, and old growth free.

For every 5,000 books printed, New Society saves the following resources:[1]

20	Trees
1,772	Pounds of Solid Waste
1,949	Gallons of Water
2,543	Kilowatt Hours of Electricity
3,221	Pounds of Greenhouse Gases
14	Pounds of HAPs, VOCs, and AOX Combined
5	Cubic Yards of Landfill Space

[1]Environmental benefits are calculated based on research done by the Environmental Defense Fund and other members of the Paper Task Force who study the environmental impacts of the paper industry.

For a full list of NSP's titles, please call 1-800-567-6772 or check out our web site at:

www.newsociety.com

NEW SOCIETY PUBLISHERS